A COMPARATIVE STUDY OF DON JUAN AND MADHYAMAKA BUDDHISM

A COMPARATIVE STUDY OF DON JUAN AND MADHYAMAKA BUDDHISM

Knowledge and Transformation

MARK MACDOWELL

MOTILAL BANARSIDASS PUBLISHERS PVT. LTD.
DELHI

First Edition: Delhi, 1981
Reprinted: Delhi, 1986, 1991

ISBN: 81-208-0162-8

Also available at:
MOTILAL BANARSIDASS
41 U.A., Bungalow Road, Jawahar Nagar, Delhi 110 007
120 Royapettah High Road, Mylapore, Madras 600 004
24 Race Course Road, Bangalore 560 001
Ashok Rajpath, Patna 800 004
Chowk, Varanasi 221 001

PRINTED IN INDIA
BY JAINENDRA PRAKASH JAIN AT SHRI JAINENDRA PRESS, A-45 NARAINA INDUSTRIAL AREA, PHASE I, NEW DELHI 110 028 AND PUBLISHED BY NARENDRA PRAKASH JAIN FOR MOTILAL BANARSIDASS PUBLISHERS PVT. LTD., BUNGALOW ROAD, JAWAHAR NAGAR, DELHI 110 007

DEDICATED TO

MY FAMILY

PREFACE

Ours is an age of much knowledge, but of much very specialized knowledge. Even in recent years we have seen a significant trend from higher education in the traditional sense (e.g. liberal arts) to a higher education in the form of technical schools and junior colleges. This trend is but an indicator of a much larger trend. The larger trend is the same in nature as the more specific one, that is, technical knowledge has been placed at center stage in our technical world. The domain of this trend is our entire world-society. No longer are just a handful of countries exposing small percentages of their population to these specific pursuits. The whole world down to the smallest nation, is immersed in a sea of technology, a sea of specifics.

It is as a counterpoint to this cultural backdrop that the present work is being offered. Don Juan, Nāgārjuna and others to be mentioned represent islands in our seas. They embody the most fundamental and, therefore, most general knowledge of the nature of things, and yet not so to the exclusion of particular knowledge which is so important for our everyday world.

Technology and specialization are not hereby being rejected; quite the contrary, they will be placed in a different perspective than the present day distorted and unhealthy views that dominate our world scene.

March 9, 1981 Mark MacDowell

PROLOGUE

Reading the four works of Castaneda about the teachings of Don Juan[1] is a journey in itself. The same can be said for the life of Nāgārjuna[2] and also for the lives of some of the Tibetan masters. But a special sort of magic arises from their study in combination. Somehow when we see such striking similarity of thought and practice which is separated so far in time and space, we cannot help but marvel at the insights and universality of both teachings.

We cannot hope to cover the topic from top to bottom in so few chapters. Actually, the material that has been dealt with in the present work is only skeletal. We hope that the bibliography furnished will give the reader some direction toward the explication of any point that is found to be interesting. There are numerous points that we have not mentioned due to lack of space Lung-gompa as described by Alexandra David-Neel[3] and others compares quite favorably with Don Juan's "gait of power.', Furthermore, the "double," as described by Ms. Neel, Lama Govinda and others, also compares favorably with the "double" as described by Don Juan's "the dreamer and the dreamed." The shapes such as the crescent and others in Don Juan's teachings can also be interpreted as tantric. There are parallels at every turn.

While we do not have the space to explore all of these vast caverns of experience, we hope that our outline can serve as a

---

1. Carlos Castaneda, *The Teachings of Don Juan : A Yaqui Way of Knowledge*. Berkeley : University of California Press, 1968.

2. Nāgārjuna, 1-2 A.D., is generally regarded as the founder of the Madhyamaka School of Buddhism, which in time became the fountainhead of Mahāyāna Buddhism, in particular in Tibetan and Zen schools of wisdom.

3. Mme. Alexandra David-Neel, a French physician and seeker of wisdom, spent several years in Tibet studying under accomplished lamas and was finally initiated into Tibetan Buddhism. *Magic and Mystery in Tibet* and *Secret Oral Teachings* are among her more well-known works on Tibet and Tibetan Buddhism.

starting point for those interested in the pursuit of the truly universal and *not* of Universal Truth.

What is it then which can be gleaned as universal from these two teachings ? The answer is not simple. The teachings of Don Juan as well as those of Nāgārjuna can be, and have been taken in a wholly negative light. It is easy to conclude from a cursory study of Nāgārjuna's dialectic that the whole enterprise culminates in despair and nihilism. The same can be said of Don Juan's "using death as an advisor." After all, when we push a given study into a pigeon hole such as nihilism, the subject is extremely easy to deal with. All we have to do is think of the pigeon hole whenever we think of the pigeon. However, both Don Juan and Nāgārjuna exude life to such a great extent that they jolt us into remembering that the pigeon does not spend absolutely all of its time in the pigeon hole. Even the pigeon remembers that it has wings and can fly. The hole is just a resting place. Yes, it is true that Don Juan and Nāgārjuna speak of death and the "emptiness" of conceptual thinking: yet they do so only to clear the path for further growth. When the student realizes that there is more to the self than conceptual thought, and more to life than death, the pigeon takes leave of its hole-bound shackle to grace the sky with the new-found wings. Once this has happened, nihilism will no longer find a home.

But how is this balance achieved ? Let us start with Nāgārjuna. The first achievement of the student studying Nāgārjuna is to master the dialectic. What the dialectic shows is this : that *any* view whatsoever if taken as *ultimately* descriptive of the world, a state of affairs, or the universe, is *necessàrily* self-contradictory. However, rather than taking the lower path which arrives at the dead end that "nothing really matters then anyhow", the bodhisattva braves the higher path of self-realization. The bodhisattva uses this analysis of views as self-contradictory as a springboard to the realization of experiences beyond language. The dialectic shocks the student *not* into a nihilistic stupor, but onto a path of action which knows no bounds.

Don Juan performs this in roughly the same way. On the one hand, the life of the warrior is fixed, rational, logical. On the other hand, Don Juan bombarded Castaneda with sensory experience for which there are no linguistic counterparts. In this way Castaneda learned that language is a part of the world, a part of experience. But neither the world nor experience can be captured by language. As Don Juan says, there is very much more to the world than language and thought, although language and thought are as integral a part of the world as anything else.

Of course there must be methods prescribed for such endeavors toward perfection, and it is obvious that both teachings have these practices; but due to the weightiness of the overall paths, the practices are only alluded to and not really detailed. This is so because Don Juan and Nāgārjuna maintain that a living teacher is necessary to steer the student clear of the myriad deadly pitfalls. Man's practically unbound seizing or clinging makes his path to freedom a path for delusion to all the most wary. According to Don Juan, the warrior's power guides him to a teacher and a benefactor. According to the Buddhist tradition, the fortitude and humility of the aspirant make possible the intersection between the karmic path of the student and that of the guru. To simply place these teachings in book form does not carry the power necessary for the student to cultivate and culminate the path. The practices without the aid of a guru are said to be downright harmful. This is not so hard to believe since the student does not really know where the path leads. How then can one plan to guide oneself across terrains filled with the most awesome and mindboggling obstacles without having the vaguest idea as to the nature of these obstacles ?

We all think of ourselves as somehow extraordinary, which in a certain sense is true; but, we should remember that from the literature available, even the most extraordinary take many years to cultivate the path. We cannot therefore assume that since we have read a few books here and there we somehow have a handle on the whole message. Nothing could be more misleading and harmful. The total paths of Don Juan and Nāgārjuna transcend talk, transcend philosophy. True, the talk and the philosophy are necessary prerequisites for higher realizations; nonetheless, there is a point where talk ends and only practice follows.

This point is constantly hinted at by scholars, but it is so obscure that even *they* don't realize it ! Russell's paradox, Godel's incompleteness proofs, Einstein's general theory of relativity all point toward experience beyond language. But since we are totally unprepared for a revelation of such staggering magnitude, we overlook these keys or hints as just momentary setbacks on man's way to stardom through intellectualism. Our intellect insists that everything be pigeonholed and who are we to stand in the way ?

Intellectualism and science, while themselves being keys to experience, are all too often the swinging medallions which produce mesmerization. We all too easily get lost in intellectual intricacies only to forget that these intricacies pale away into simplistic reductionism in the light of possible experience.

Think of the last time that you ran out of milk just as you were nestling into your favorite chair readying yourself for the enjoyment of your favorite cookies. Since the cookies could not possibly have been enjoyed without the companion milk, a fast trip to the store was necessary. On the way, literally thousands upon thousands of things happened. First of all, the motion of our step by step walking induces our eyes into envisioning the environment in an up and down motion. We walk to and past innumerable objects, houses, trees, birds, insects, pavements, signs and so on. Further, these objects are far from simple. When we stop to analyse, the smallest of houses and the humblest of flora are incredibly complicated. We hear thousands of sounds and have literally hundreds of thousands of sensations of smell, sight, hearing, touch and taste. Were we to try to correlate all of the points on all the trees and all of the points on all of the houses and so on with our motion in walking, we incur disaster.

First, the mathematical description would be so unwieldy as to produce volumes of equations for only small fragments of our experience. The description of our sensory motion with respect to our entire environment is quite literally impossible. But let this not worry us since, after all, we are human beings, and as such we are capable of having all of these experiences. Even if we could somehow collect mathematical formulations for such experience, the equations would be no substitute for the experience itself.

And yet, much to our shame, when we arrive back from the store, if we were asked what happened on our trip to the store, we would probably reply, "Oh, nothing". The trip to the store was overlooked in our haste for the early enjoyment of milk and cookies. The trip was merely a necessary evil on our way to stomach gratification. Our evening is reduced to running to the store, coming home gobbling down milk and cookies, watching the football game, and finally snoozing off into sleepsville. An infinity of experience is at our beck and call. Unfortunately we constantly miss and miss again literally infinite experience. We miss it because our world is reduced to milk, cookies, and television.

If an insignificant trip to the store holds infinity before us, what then is yielded by a lifetime of our ramblings? Potentially much, but all too often nothing. We become all too consumed and entranced by the pigeon holes which we erect for ourselves and then squeeze into.

We lose infinity upon infinity of experience because we cannot uncling from milk and cookies and pigeon holes. We are so entranced by our likings (or clingings) that they overshadow other experience. The other possible experiences are overshadowed to such a degree that we offhandedly reject them as insignificant. Our intellect forces us to forget that the level of significance of any event is determined by us. There is no tableau in the sky which is inscribed with "milk and cookies are almost the most important things". We think that these things are important, and in our enthusiasm we blot out thousands of other experiences. We find ourselves in this ignoble circumstance because of clinging. The Miami Dolphins are important and therefore we miss the message of a beautiful moonset. It happens all the time and yet we go on sleeping.

But even this analogy of sleeping is not wholly appropriate. After all, when we sleep, we dream; and in dreams, anything can happen. Not so in our daily lives. In our daily lives, only those things can happen which we include as co-occupants of our pigeon hole. Often times we get bored, even bored to such an extent that we increase the number of co-occupants of our pigeon hole. But no matter how many objects, events, or activities with which we identify, simply the inclusion of those objects, events, or activities, automatically excludes many thousands times other experiences.

The trick is not to identify with any particular aspect of phenomena. This frees us to enjoy the individuality and yet the ultimate commonality with *all* of experience. Being tied to nothing means the enjoyment of all. This of course is the object of practices espoused by Don Juan, Nāgārjuna and others by way of non-egotism and mindfulness.

Without these practices our intellect reduces our experience to a dead skeleton. With these practices, our world becomes a living, breathing organism which communicates with us every micro-second of the day. All we have to do is to listen.

* * * *

But how do we listen to the world communicate ? We can only communicate with an object, or array of objects, when we feel that we are on a par with them. When this happens, that is, when we don't feel any more important than the ant or the tree or the doorknob, we are attuned to the slightest fluctuations in the phenomenal as well as the non-linguistic aspect of ants, and trees, and so on. These fluctuations are actually minute interactions of the "nagual."[1] The fluctuations are actually in the mind, since the entire cosmos is generated from the mind. Living the life of the warrior or bodhisattva enables us to attune ourselves to the world and therefore our own subtle selves. When the mind is empty, only power exists (although this view is ultimately self-contradictory). When we phase from emptiness or power into conceptual activity, we can see the roots of the universe and therefore the roots of ourselves. Equating ourselves with other objects of the universe does not "drag us down to their level," but "pulls us up to their level". The earth communicates with us and we communicate with it.

It is very easy, however, to formulate these views and utter banalities about communicating with nature. The actual

1. Nagual is the non-conceptual, non-perceptual reality (power) that manifests itself as the myriad of phenomena. Nagual is nameless, formless, unthinkable, untalkable, and unimaginable. It is the void from which arise all existents.

practice of the no-nonsense attitude of not considering ourselves any better than the most insignificant corner of the universe while not falling into the depression of the loss of all self-respect, requires an impeccable balancing of the "tonal"[1] and "nagual" that the highest effort is required of both student and teacher. This can be done only when each recognizes that their karmas are in the appropriate configurations. When this happens, the student is in a position to walk the dangerous passageway to perfection. The teacher never gives anything that is not asked for by the student. This is why the student must be mentally tight, and karmically aware in order to avert certain default. The signpost on the path is so utterly unfamiliar that the unguided and overconfident stumble off into oblivion before anyone suspects danger. This is no haughty warning from "someone who knows," but rather a humble observation by one who has done limited research on these matters.

1. Tonal : is conventional, ordinary descriptions of the world; these descriptions are always from the point of view of some conceptual-perceptual framework or other. In a word, Tonal is phenomena.

CONTENTS

Chapter I

INTRODUCTION

In Western philosophy, and thereby in Western life, there has been a separation, namely that between the mind and the body. The dichotomy is not a natural state of affairs, but is produced by viewing the world through dualistic categories. One might ask, "How is this possible ?" We shall answer this question in the sequel.

It is the purpose of this book to address this question in light of relatively new information[1] of occurrences in our own Western world. Until recently it has seemed that to escape the philosophy of mind-body dualism (and thereby all allegedly ultimate dualism) we have had to look to the East. Not that this is any sort of a distasteful task, but until now we are hard pressed to find a Western parallel to Buddhist philosophy. Part of the purpose of the present work is to show that such a parallel is to be found in the four works of Carlos Castaneda.

Castaneda in the early and mid-sixties was a graduate student in the field of sociology. His interest in certain social phenomena led him to Arizona and Mexico where he "studied," in a manner of speaking not just social phenomena, but phenomena

1. The author is fully aware of the doubts cast by certain reviewers and commentators on the authenticity of not only Castaneda's discipleship under Don Juan but also the very existence of Don Juan himself as a historical personality. Such doubts have no bearing on the task of the present work. The reason for this is that we are not concerned here with historical matters; rather our concern is with concepts and ideas, which, in the author's judgment, are the only things of consequence to any philosophical study. It is worth pointing out here that there are many philosophical works in both East and West, particularly in the former, which are hailed as masterpieces but of whose authorship we are completely ignorant. The point is that the historical existence (or lack thereof) of these sources of idea has no bearing on the truth and value of those ideas.

in general. That is to say that Castaneda was introduced to a "man of Knowledge" of American Indian descent.

During the course of Castaneda's apprenticeship he bore witness to fantastic events, impossible and indescribable by our ordinary categories, and only spoken of in terms of colorful metaphor. The culmination of these experiences is described in *Tales of Power*.[1]

We are extremely fortunate that the teachings of Castaneda's gurus (Don Juan and Don Genaro as he calls them) are related in a beautiful fashion by Castaneda.

Some time in the course of Castaneda's apprenticeship he brought to Don Juan a copy of Evans-Wentz' book, *The Tibetan Book of the Dead* (*Bardo Thodol*).[2] He querried Don Juan about it, wondering whether or not there were grounds of comparison between Don Juan's teachings and those of the *Bardo Thodol*. Don Juan passed the question over lightly, probably because those teachings did not have an immediate bearing on Castaneda's life as did his own. However, Don Juan did mention that the people espousing those teachings were capable of some of the same realizations of *his* way of life. The matter was thereby dropped.

The main purpose of this book, then, is to explore the parallels between the teachings of Don Juan and those of non-Western philosophies—in particular Buddhism, as expounded by Nāgārjuna in his Madhyamaka (Middle way) philosophy.

The Madhyamaka school was founded by Nāgārjuna around the second century A.D.,[3] as a reaction to the controversy between Sarvâstivâdins and Mahâsaṅghikas, concerning the ontological status of dharmas (ultimate constituents of reality), the former maintaining that dharmas have duration and the latter that dharmas are unequivocally governed by the instantaneous theory of being (doctrine of momentariness "kṣaṇika-vâda").[4]

1. Carlos Castaneda, *Tales of Power* (New York: Simon and Schuster, 1974).

2. W.Y. Evans-Wentz, *The Tibetan Book of the Dead* (Oxford University Press, 1960).

3. Ramanan places his activity between 50 and 120 A.D.

4. Junjiro Takakusu, *The Essentials of Buddhist Philosophy* (Honolulu: Office Appliance Co., Ltd., 1956), Ch. IV, pp. 57-73.

Nāgārjuna's teaching is the Middle Way, not because he teaches some sort of mathematical average of these or any other extremes (such as eternalism and annihilationism, self and non-self, matter and spirit, body and soul, substance and process, unity and plurality, identity and difference), but because he espouses non-clinging to any extreme, thereby steering clear of conflict and dogmatism, which are the source of dukkha (suffering). During the course of this book, we shall investigate the implications of this avoidance of extremes.

We began this introduction by calling attention to the mind-body dichotomy which has shaped the philosophy of life in the Western world. The uncritical and hence dogmatic view that since we have absolute constituents of language (or analysis), there must be, correspondingly, absolute constituents of reality, Western man has created his insoluble problems, philosophic as well as religious. According to Nāgārjuna, the source of these problems is the mistaking of the ultimates of analysis for the ultimates of the real.[1] Philosophically (as if there could be another way) the mind-body problem has puzzled thinkers for centuries. But no matter how the argumentation proceeds, the outcome is always the same, that is, there is a problem. But the fact that there is a problem at all is disquieting and is indicative of some division and fragmentation, the breeding ground of doubt and uncertainty and thereby of pain and suffering.

With respect to the mundane (the empirical), it is because we cling to the view that the world is constituted of bodies and minds that we ignore one or the other, thereby valuing sheer intellectualism or sheer hedonism in an exclusive manner. As regards the transmundane, our refusal to abolish dichotomies as absolutes stands in our way of abolishing not only the schism between mind and body, but ultimately the schism between self and world. One of the major tasks of this book will be an exposition of the absurdity as well as the vacuity of all extremes, as shown both in the philosophy of Nāgārjuna and in the teachings of Don Juan.

---

1. K. Venkata Ramanan, *Nāgārjuna's Philosophy as Presented in the Mahā-Prajñāpāramitā-Śāstra* (Bharatiya Vidya Prakashan, 1971), p. 65.

Nāgārjuna teaches that to prefer one extreme of a duality over another would be to completely ignore their essential unity. One might ask, "What essential unity?" This point will be discussed at length in Chapter 2; but for the present, suffice it to mention that according to Nāgārjuna clinging to either extreme of any dichotomy necessarily forces one into ignoring the essential unity (i.e. relativity) of the pairs, e.g. hot and cold, high and low—any C and non-C in general. In doing so, we open the way for alienation from views opposed to ours and, therefore, ultimately for alienation between the self and the world (non-self). According to Nāgārjuna, the root cause of all alienation is the thinking of ourselves as being separate, isolated entities—the so-called self-existent entities.

Nāgārjuna does not deny that the mind is separate from the body as any more (or less) true than the mind being one with the body. He only wishes to show the dependence of one upon the other in reference to the phenomenal. Both are views, but they are not ultimate *truths*. To cling to either would be a mistake. The phenomenal is conditioned; that is, we cannot speak of the one (mind *or* body) in the absence of the other. Although we only 'see' bodies, we can hardly make sense of the world without referring to minds. Both bodies *and* minds have an empirical reality but to deny one for the other is a mistake, whether the denier be a hedonist, an intellectual, or an ascetic. But the unity of mind and body does not in any sense require us to ignore the *pragmatic efficacy* of speaking of minds and bodies:

> To him who would cling to the determination of no 'I' (and mine), and would say that this alone is true and the rest is false, one should indeed object. "According to you, in the true nature of things there is no I, and so how can you say, 'I have heard . . .'?"[1]

To deny totally the "I" is to deny it even as a relative truth. Likewise, the total denial of the mind-body dichotomy would be to deny it as a relative truth.

1. K. Venkata Ramanan, *Nāgārjuna's Philosophy as Presented in the Mahā-Prajñāpāramitā-Śāstra* (Bharatiya Vidya Prakashan, 1971), p. 104.

Nâgârjuna refers to this mutual dependence as "conditioned origination." Just as the seed and eventually the tree is dependent upon the sun, the earth, the water, and so on, and each of these upon others, then, too, a category such as mind is dependent upon the one of body and vice versa. It is equally important to note that even the view in which mind and body are not separate is dependent upon that in which they are separate.

We shall detail these discussions later, but for now we merely wish to draw attention to one of the main insights of the Madhyamaka philosophy: on the phenomenal level, self-existence is denied. This simply means that there is nothing in the phenomenal world that remains unchanging and permanent. Hence the doctrine of dependent origination: "This arising that arises, this ceasing to be that ceases to be." When one takes a "still frame" of this continuum then substances and attributes arise. Substance and attribute are at the logical, analytic level. Phenomena are simply the course of conditionally originating and perishing impingements upon the senses.

On the analytic level, substance and attribute arise hand in hand, each existing precisely because the other does, consequently, to say that the world is ultimately composed of substance(s) clearly leads to contradictions. On the other hand, to cling to process as the real is likewise to be trapped into contradictions. These points will be expanded and explained in due course in the discussion of Nâgârjuna's dialectic.

The same points are made by Don Juan in his teaching to Castaneda. Don Juan exhorts Castaneda to stop viewing the world through the categories to which he is accustomed. Toward the end of *Separate Reality*[1] Don Juan recalls to Castaneda that he (the latter) had once told him that wise men of his tradition had said that in the infinity of time no moment was ever repeated. Castaneda admitted that he had said this, and still held it to be the case. Whereupon, Don Juan advised him to fix his gaze upon a certain leaf of a tree. The leaf fell, striking certain portions of the tree, and finally the ground. Don Juan directed

1. Carlos Castaneda, *A Separate Reality* (New York : Simon and Schuster, 1971), p. 259 ff.

him to look again. The same event transpired. Upon further and closer inspection the same event repeated itself over and over.

How Don Juan effected this is not of immediate concern to us. What does concern us is that merely by doing so Don Juan jolted Castaneda into the realization that since analysis necessitates our looking at events as though they are in principle unrepeatable, we actually believe the world to be structured in that way. Such a realization made clear to Castaneda the possibilities of "other worlds."

What we have been alluding to in the foregoing pages is this: there are definite parallels between the teachings of Don Juan and Nāgārjuna. While we have briefly referred to some of the important parallels, namely that the root cause of suffering lies in our compulsive tendency to look for absolute truth and absolute reality, Castaneda's books abound in even more far-reaching similarities with the teachings of Nāgārjuna. In this book, we hope to trace the similarities from top to bottom, that is, from metaphysics and epistemology through logic, psychology, and finally ethics.

The propriety of such an undertaking seems to be plain enough. We find that these two philosophies (ultimately ways of life) are so similar despite their vast spatio-temporal separation. The concepts seem to leap so fantastically over cultural bounds that one's imagination and curiosity are deeply stirred. Curiosity, not about the actual mechanics of tracing their origins to a possible common source (although this is a distinct possibility), but about the teachings themselves.

While people have searched for universal truth, e.g. the universal criterion in Kant's ethics, there is something that is truly universal about the teachings of Don Juan and Nāgārjuna. Their observations on man's relationship with the world have lept boundaries of space, time and culture. Nāgārjuna's observations on human nature in 2nd century India are astoundingly similar to those of Don Juan, a man of Knowledge in 20th century America.

The cornerstone of Nāgārjuna's teachings is his dialectic leading to śūnyatā (emptiness). In order to systematically uncover more and deeper similarities between the two courses of study, we will at times refer to the lives and lessons of other sages, saints and Buddhas. The lives and teachings of such masters as Naropa, Tilopa, and Milerapa are profound and extraordinary testimony to the practical (or ethical) consequences of the intellectual insights of Nāgārjuna's dialectic. The whole of these teachings will then be a better topic of comparison, since Don Juan did not divide his teachings into separate topics such as logic, metaphysics, etc.

Hopefully, by studying both of these teachings in their own contexts we will come to a better understanding of their basic insights and surely of ourselves and of the at once familiar and mysterious world we inhabit.

Chapter II

THE MADHYAMAKA

Most books that are not exclusively concerned with Madhyamaka do not refer to Nāgārjuna outside of the dialectic. It is the intention of this chapter to discuss the dialectic, look at some of its applications, and then to carry its implications from the strictly formal to the experiential. Accordingly, we shall first present an overview of Nāgārjuna's Madhyamaka philosophy in enough detail for us to refer back to it in later chapters when we need to draw specific parallels between the Madhyamaka and the teachings of Don Juan.

Some of the following analyses would be difficult to come by were it not for the insightful works of T.R.V. Murti[1] and K. Venkata Ramanan.[2] All students of Madhyamaka philosophy are much indebted to these scholars for their definitive treatises.

When one notes the relentless exactitude of the Madhyamaka dialectic, one could easily draw the conclusion that the dialectic is the path of knowledge. As with all other views, there is undeniably a kernel of truth to this. But what makes this view misleading is the word "knowledge." If we think that by "knowledge" is meant discursive knowledge, then the statement is surely misleading. As such, it is best to understand "knowledge" here in the sense of prajñā (wisdom).

Let us note immediately that unlike Zeno's dialectic, Nāgārjuna's does not strive to show that, for example, motion is impossible and thereby conclude that only rest is characteristic of the real. Quite the contrary, in the Madhyamaka everything that follows

1. T.R.V. Murti, *The Central Philosophy of Buddhism* (London: Allen and Unwin, 1960).

2. K. Venkata Ramanan, *Nāgārjuna's Philosophy as Presented in the Mahā-Prajñāpāramitā-Śāstra* (Bharatiya Vidya Prakashan, 1971).

the dialectic's having laid bare all dichotomy as śūnyatā (empty) is nondiscursive. In other words, the dialectic is not an argumentative tool used to bolster one's own biases. The dialectic exposes with equal vigor the inherent inconsistencies in both sides of an issue. The dialectic reveals in clear detail exactly where antinomies lie in wait for the unwary.

The dialectic is only the beginning for the farer of the Middle path. One does not follow the dialectic to the end only to rest upon one's intellectual achievements. As Murti puts it, the dialectic is a catharsis.[1] It exoterically makes us aware of the conflicts in reason. What follows then is esoteric. That is, once the dialectic has pointed the way by showing the absurdity and intellectual vacuity of apologizing for a particular point of view, esoterically the way-farer stops clinging to particular views as extensions of the ego and sees them for what they are. Phenomenologically, one's world expands, not only incorporating the discursive as part and parcel of man's existence, but also including the nondiscursive vastness to which our categories do not and cannot come close to touching. The categories do not *approximate* reality, not because they are too simple, but because they are the products of particular perceptual-conceptual activities. This is another way of saying that sensation and intellection color a topography across the real. In short, the real is indeterminate:

> The Madhyamaka method is to deconceptualize the mind and to disburden it of all notions, empirical as well as a priori . . . [2]

In this way, the empirical and the a priori are the same in that they are both products of intellection.

> It is primarily a path of purification of the intellect . . . The method is negative. Universality and certitude are reached not by the summation of particular points of view, but by rigidly excluding them; for a view is always particular . . . It is not nihilism, which is a standpoint asserting that nothing

1. T.R.V. Murti, *The Central Philosophy of Buddhism* (London: Allen and Unwin, 1960), p. 212.

2. ibid., p. 212.

> is. The dialectic is the rejection of all views including the nihilistic.
>
> The implication of the Madhyamaka method is that the real is overlaid with the undergrowth of our notions and views. Most of them are a priori; this is 'avidyā,' which, in this is equated with ideal construction screening the real.[1]

This is a good point at which to present the method and structure of the dialectic itself. The dialectic is the exoteric counterpart of the esoteric, phenomenological prajñā-pāramitā (intuitional insight). While the dialectic lays bare the dichotomies of language and perception, prajñā-pāramitā melts the phenomenal distinctions that we make, thereby uncovering the real.

> Even in the Vedānta and the Vijñānavāda, the dialectic is in the service of a theory of the real which these systems uphold. Only in the Madhyamaka is the dialectic not a means but an end. Criticism itself is philosophy.[2]

In the Western tradition and in certain schools of Indian philosophy, dialectic assumes the following form:

1) P (proposition to be proven)
2) Assume $\sim P$
3) .
.) .
.) .
.) . χ
K+1) $\sim \chi$
K+2) $\therefore$ P

In contrast, Nāgārjuna's dialectic takes the following form:

1) P (proposition)	1A) $\sim P$ (proposition)
2) Assume P	2A) Assume $\sim P$

1. T.R.V. Murti, *The Central Philosophy of Buddhism* (London: Allen and Unwin, 1960), p. 212.
2. ibid., p. 213.

3) :	3^{A}) :
: :	:
K) χ	K^{A}) χ^{A}
K+1) $\sim\chi$	$K^{A}+1$) $\sim\chi^{A}$

The above schema clearly shows that for the Mādhyamika, unlike for Zeno, the demonstration of the absurdity (reductio ad absurdum) of a thesis does not warrant the claim of the truth of its negation. Thus, according to the Mādhyamika, Zeno's demonstration of the absurdity of motion does not entail the thesis of rest. For one can show that the thesis of rest also leads to a contradiction.

In order to illustrate the actual workings of the dialectic, we shall apply it to the concept of causation. Nāgārjuna's dialectic has four logical alternatives concerning any thesis in general. Simply put, they are:

1) S is Q
2) S is $\sim$Q
3) S is both Q and $\sim$Q
4) S is neither Q nor $\sim$Q

Alternatives 1 and 2 are generally sufficient for the discussion of most or all of Western philosophy while all four facets are used in the discussion of non-Western philosophy.[1]

1. The reason for this lies in the fact that the law of excluded middle as formulated by Aristotle occupies a central place in Western thought in general and logic in particular. Thus it is easy to see that for a thinker in the Western tradition alternatives 1 and 2 are the only possibilities. This is another way of saying that alternatives 3 and 4 are ruled out by the principle of excluded middle. In contrast, the Madhyamika recognizes the four alternatives as mutually exclusive and jointly exhaustive. It is to be noted that while the Mādhymika, like Western thinkers, recognizes the principle of non-contradiction he does not, unlike Western thinkers, accept the law of excluded middle without qualification. He recognizes the law of excluded middle in cases where the alternatives are shown to be finite and mutually exclusive, but not in contexts where there is no warranty to think that such is the case. As will be seen presently, the Mādhyamika considers the principle of excluded middle valid in purely logical-mathematical contexts, but not in the context of ontology, which is the prime concern of philosophy.

In his analysis of his antinomies, Kant starts with the disjunctive form, A is either P or ~P, which is none other than the legal combination of facets 1 and 2 of Nāgārjuna's dialectic. Each antinomy is expressed in the form: thesis (A is P) and antithesis (A is ~P), and discussion thereof. In general, what Kant does is consider the thesis, assume the antithesis, and find a logical contradiction in the antithesis, thereby proving the thesis. Then he considers the antithesis, assumes the thesis, likewise generates a contradiction, thereby proving the antithesis. Schematically,

I		II	
1)	A is P	1)	A is ~P
2)	assume A is ~P	2)	assume A is P
3)	:	3)	:
.)	.	.)	.
.)	.	.)	.
.)	.	.)	.
K)	χ	K)	χ^1
K+1)	$\sim\chi$	K+1)	$\sim\chi^1$
K+2)	∴ A is P	K+2)	∴ A is ~P

Combining I and II, Kant arrives at A is P and A is ~P, a contradiction, Kantian antinomy. From this Kant concludes that in regard to the subject matter of the antinomies reason breaks down and, what is worse, produces transcendental illusions. It is worth noting that while Kant applies this analysis only in the context of antinomies, Nāgārjuna applies the dialectic to any statement, dichotomy or abstraction—in general any thesis whatever concerning reality. Kant resolves the antinomies by asserting that both thesis and antithesis are beyond the purview of reason. This does not mean, however, that he establishes one or the other as true, but only forces them to inhabit the same sphere. He accomplishes this in the first antinomy with the introduction of the distinction between "infinite regress" and "indeterminately continued regress."[1]

1. N.K. Smith, trans. *Critique of Pure Reason*, by Immanuel Kant (New York: St. Martin's Press, 1965), p. 455.

Nāgārjuna's prasaṅga (reductio ad absurdum) on the other hand, is quite different from Kant's dialectic of the antinomies. Nāgārjuna assumes the thesis and generates a contradiction immediately from itself.

1) A is P
2) :
3)
K) χ
K+1) $\sim\chi$

The difference lies herein: Thus Kant would claim that therefore 'A is $\sim$ P' is the case, Nāgārjuna makes no such claim. He simply lets the contradiction stand as testimony to the 'emptiness' of any concept or category when claimed 'absolute' and 'exclusive.' Nāgārjuna would then cement his discussion by showing contradictions in the cases of A is $\sim$ P, A is both P and $\sim$ P, and A is neither P nor $\sim$ P. By this digression, we hope to distinguish the Mādhyamika conception of 'prasaṅga' (reductio ad absurdum) from other forms of reductio ad absurdum which *seem* to be either the same as or similar to it. The chief difference is this: while other dialectics (e.g. Kant's) use the reductio to posit a positive statement about the world (i.e. generate a metaphysics), Nāgārjuna's prasaṅga systematically refrains from asserting any thesis. Further, the prasaṅga of Nāgārjuna does not limit the choice of alternatives to the dictates of the principle of the excluded middle. On the contrary, it allows for different sorts of world views in its inclusion of the propositions (3) and (4) listed above, namely, "A is both P and $\sim$ P" and "A is neither P nor $\sim$ P", respectively. Let us illustrate the workings of the Madhyamaka dialectic with regard to one of Kant's antinomies.

The First Antinomy:

Thesis: The world has a beginning in time, and is also limited as regards space (A is P).

Antithesis: The world has no beginning in time, and no limits in space; it is infinite as regards both time and space (A is $\sim$ P).[1]

1. N.K. Smith, trans. *Critique of Pure Reason,* by Immanuel Kant (New York: St. Martin's Press, 1965), p. 396.

Let us consider the thesis. If the world is limited in space, then what is the nature of this limit? Is it an "other" to the world? If the limit is other than the world, then what effect would it have on the world? If it is other than the world, what relation could obtain between the world and the limit? Is this limit the same as the world or part of it? If this were the case, then it certainly would be no boundary at all. Where would its limiting power be?

One could prolong the argument by saying that like the fence that straddled a property line, part is on one side, and part is on the other side of the line. This might work well in surveying properties, but if we say part of the limit belongs to the world, then where does the other part belong? It certainly does not belong to empty space. Further, how could one delineate between that part of the boundary which is part of the world, and that which is not?

What about beginning in time? For the world to have a beginning in time, the existence of time prior to the world would be necessary. Yet, what meaning does time have in the absence of change in the world? Certainly time and change are mutually dependent concepts. Speaking of one without the other is impossible. Therefore, how could the world have a beginning in time?

This is, of course, not to imply that the world does not have a beginning in time. Thus let us consider the antithesis. If the world has no limits in space, then what is it that we are referring to as the world? Is it this tree plus that sky plus that ground? Is it the earth, the solar system, the galaxie? We speak of what we see as though it were part of a whole. But what then is the whole? Having no limits in space would imply that the world is infinite.

But how can we refer to something as infinite? It seems a difficult problem since we would speak of the world in comparison to what? The world would be left dangling as a concept since there is nothing to cast it in opposition with. We see the picture on the wall, not just as a picture, but as a picture contrasted against the wall. In order to conceptualize something (i.e. to enumerate the constitutive and individuating principles by which we categorize objects and events),[1] we need to give those properties by virtue of which an object is categorizable as such-and-such, as well as those properties which make that event distinct from all other events within that category. If the world is infinite, it would be the only object in that category; as such, it is difficult to see how we could even begin to speak of the world in such circumstances.

And what about time ? Time and change are mutually dependent categories. We can speak of time only in terms of change and change in terms of time. It is clear then that if the world had a beginning, time would have to transcend the world. But to what then would time be in reference ? It is clear that time is empty, save for the mutual dependence between it and change in the realm of the phenomenal.

Could the world then be infinite with respect to time ? That is, does the world have neither a beginning nor end in time? If we accept this view, then time too would be infinite, being directly tied to change and the world. One might say that time is a sort of a distance between one event and another. But if this "distance" were infinite, then the concept of distance collapses since the traversing of this distance is impossible by virtue of its being infinite. An infinite amount of time is like no time at all, since the conceptualization of change and the world are impossible in either case. As a matter of fact, we can only think and speak of time pragmatically. Forgetting this we mistakenly give these categories an ultimate status (absolute and exclusive).

The above analysis is not wholly different from Kant's. This discussion was merely to introduce Nāgārjuna's dialectic on more familiar grounds. We shall now present Nāgārjuna's application of prasaṅga to the concept of causality.

Historically, the prasaṅga was invoked upon four views of causality. Following our format, satkāryavāda (identity between cause and effect) is held by the Sāṁkhya schools; and Asatkāryavāda (difference between cause and effect) is held by some Buddhist schools and the Nyāya-Vaiśeṣika. Trying to bridge the gap

1. S. Korner, *Categorical Frameworks* (New York: Barnes and Noble, Inc., 1970), p. 7 et passim.

between complete identity and complete difference the Jaina school mechanically joins asatkāryavāda and satkāryavāda together (S is Q *and* S is not Q). Rejecting all these points of view, the materialist (Cārvāka) opts for chance production, the fourth alternative, i.e. S is neither Q nor ~Q.

The Sāṁkhya argues that while the appearance (form) of the effect is certainly different from the cause, cause and effect are identical in substance. But even with this cautious phraseology, the Sāṁkhya cannot bolster his argument for identity without reference to difference. If the silica were completely identical with the pane of glass, then why is it that we cannot see through silica? Why should the Sāṁkhya arbitrarily draw a line and say that on this side of the line, where substance resides, there is identity, and therefore, claim identity between cause and effect? Why is it that to the Sāṁkhya substance is more basic, more indicative of the real than attribute? After all, can one speak of substance without referring to attribute? Where does one encounter substance without its constant companion, namely, attribute? Substance and attribute are two mutually dependent categories. One without the other is unthinkable. Similarly, absolute identity (identity without reference to difference), is unthinkable.

> Absolute identity is not even assertible. Even to affirm A is A, we have to take the help of difference of time, place and circumstances of A's occurrences etc.[1]

It is noteworthy that Murti has a further insight pertaining to this that will be helpful in later chapters. He says:

> A critique of the Sāṁkhya reveals the inner fissure present in its thesis, and in removing the inconsistency we reach an inexpressible absolute identity. We have not the right to call it an identity even. It is beyond thought, outside the range of predication.[2]

---

1. T.R.V. Murti, *The Central Philosophy of Buddhism* (London: Allen and Unwin, 1960), p. 133.
2. ibid.

The Sāṁkhya view is unacceptable because it does not admit that, while sameness or oldness is present in the effect, so is newness or difference. Absolute identity breaks down.

At the opposite end of the analysis lies the Nyāya-Vaiśeṣika. It is their contention that cause and effect are wholly different. But this Nāgārjuna would say, is a total denial of causality. After all, if two things are absolutely different from each other, how can any relation obtain between them at all ? If cause and effect are absolutely different, one should be able to produce anything from anything. Recall the above discussion of the world and its boundaries. If the boundary is totally an "other" to the world, how could it have any binding power with respect to the world ? Similarly, if cause and effect are totally different, why are we even speaking of them in conjunction ?

The Nyāya-Vaiśeṣika fails because while recognizing some degree of difference between cause and effect, they mistakenly hold that it is an absolute difference, thereby excluding and ignoring the continuous aspect of causality. There may be difference and sameness between cause and effect, but when absolutized, they generate contradictions. Cause and effect are relative, mutually dependent categories each of whose life and breath come from the very existence of the other. As Ramanan puts it, both views are guilty of mistaking the ultimates of analysis for the ultimates of reality.[1] We do not have to deny hereby the phenomenal efficacy of cause and effect, or their identity or difference. All that is denied is their *ultimacy*. Our pain and discomfort come not from analysis, but from our clinging to the analysis.

The Jaina tries to solve the problem with an eclecticism of combining these two views into the third alternative, namely, effect is both the same as and different from cause. In doing so the Jaina opens himself to all the above criticisms directed at both satkāryavāda and asatkāryavāda and more. The Jaina by combining identity and difference gains a valuable insight into the essential character of conceptualization; that is, that all

1. K. Venkata Ramanan, *Nāgārjuna's Philosophy as Presented in the Mahā-Prajñāpāramitā-Śāstra* (Bharatiya Vidya Prakashan, 1971), p. 181.

views are relative and that concepts too are relative, and hence are mutually existent. What the Jainas fail to realize is that even this view, i.e. the view that all concepts, truths, etc., are relative, is dependent itself upon some absolute or other. The Jaina seems to think that we can somehow construct the real by synthesizing partial truths. This is misleading, for they fail to regard relativism itself as relative. They cannot speak of relativity as characterizing the real without reference to some absolute. Thus by absolutizing the relative they render their position vulnerable. Whether this absolute be real or not, it cannot be ignored as the complement of the relative in conceptual analysis. "Absolute" and "relative" are two mutually dependent concepts, neither being indicative of the real.

According to the Mādhyamika, the proposition that all views and concepts are relative is a lower truth. The higher truth is the insight that this view itself is relative.

The fourth position in our format is that of the Cārvāka (school of Indian materialism). It is the view that cause is neither identical to nor different from effect (effects are neither attached nor are they not attached to causes, but arise randomly). If this view is merely asserted without supporting arguments, it fails on grounds of dogmatism. On the other hand, if the materialist wants to avoid dogmatism, he has to formulate an argument. Then, as Murti puts it:

> If a reason is assigned, there is a manifest self contradiction between what we assert and how we assert it: for we have a conclusion (that things are produced at random without cause) sought to be cogently, causally, derived from premises.[1]

This is a sketch of the Mādhyamika analysis of causality. In its fuller and detailed articulation finer distinctions are made; and at each step it becomes increasingly clear that each of these views, taken absolutely and exclusively, leads to self-contradiction. This dialectic can be applied in like fashion to any

1. T.R.V. Murti, *The Central Philosophy of Buddhism* (London: Allen and Unwin, 1960), p. 135.

and all dualities of thought and perception, for they are all mutually dependent concepts, including substance and attribute, real and unreal, motion and rest, self and non-self, relative and absolute, etc.

The dialectic, therefore, is a tool used for showing views to be what they are, relative statements about the real. It develops no positive theory of the real. For this reason, the criticism is sometimes leveled that the Mādhyamika is nihilistic, in the sense of denial of reality. But, as mentioned earlier, nihilism itself is a view, and Nāgārjuna does not endorse nihilism.

> What does it mean to deny reality? Denial of causation can entail the denial of reality only on the supposition that reality is constituted of causes and effects; and unless and until this supposition is shown to be true, Nāgārjuna cannot be charged with denying reality. What Nāgārjuna demonstrates by his dialectical critique of the concept of causation is precisely the untenability of the assumption that reality is constituted of causes and effects. Thus the import of the Mādhyamika critique is not the denial of reality, but only the denial that the concepts of cause and effect have any absolute referents in reality, for any claim that they do is self-contradictory. It is this point that is expressed by Nāgārjuna when he says that concepts are empty and void (śūnya). It is worth emphasizing that emptiness of concepts does not entail the emptiness of reality.[1]

Rather, the Mādhyamika uses the dialectic as a tool with which to chop away the underbrush, in which we only too easily get stuck, in order to clear the path for a non-clinging life.

The dialectic is a necessity in the life of the Bodhisattva because it exposes the warp and weft of conceptual knowledge. Reality is simply to be experienced. Such an experience is called "prajñāpāramitā" (intuitional insight):

> Prajñā is not a special faculty depending on causes and conditions; it is the intellect freed of conceptual restrictions

1. R. Puligandla, *An Introduction to Eastern Thought* (Nashville: Abingdon Press, 1975), p. 93.

> by the negative function of the dialectic; it is the prius of all functions, and is the universal nature of the mind.[1]

In later chapters we will investigate this "universal nature of the mind" in the teachings of Don Juan.

Thus dialectic, viewed in the context of Nāgārjuna's teachings will not lead to absolutistic views such as it does in the advaita system (viz. the dialectic is employed in the "proof" of the real as being unchanging). Quite the contrary, the dialectic, when understood properly, is a tool which frees us from all absolutist views, thereby leading to non-clinging. It is worth noting that clinging has its source in ignorance (avidyā) as to the nature of views.

To the holder of a particular view, avidyā consists in someone else's non-realization that his view is the true one. Thus to the monist, those suffering from avidyā are the pluralists; and to the pluralist, the monist is incurably ignorant. To Nāgārjuna, both are victims of avidyā, not because they do not agree with him, but because they dogmatically claim absolute and exclusive truth to their own views. The overcoming of avidyā, then, does not consist of abandoning one view for another, the allegedly true one. Rather, avidyā is overcome only when the world is experienced without the encumbrance of any view whatsoever.

> If the apprehension of the impermanent as permanent is illusion, why is the apprehension of the indeterminate as impermanent not illusion as well.[2]

So, conceptualization is the source of avidyā rather than some concept or view in concrete, although it is particular concepts to which men, in their ignorance, cling.

What, then, comes of this negative dialectic ? The immediate result is that the Mādhyamika is all accommodating. By this we mean that the Mādhyamika, unlike dogmatists, excludes

---

1. T.R.V. Murti, *The Central Philosophy of Buddhism* (London: Allen and Unwin, 1960), p. 213.

2. *Mādhyamika Kārikās of Nāgārjuna.* Ed. by L. de la V. Poussin (Bib. Budd. IV), p. 14.

no views; and with no particular view held as ultimate, he fully recognizes that he may freely choose from various metaphysical frameworks in order to deal with the phenomenal world (saṁvṛti). One realizes that all views are relative in the light of the ultimate, inexpressible, paramārtha. As a result of this realization, the farer of the middle way is able to traverse life's path without temptation or animosity towards one view or the other. In this manner, the farer of the middle way is one of infinite patience, which is none other than an existential exemplification of freedom from dogmatism and clinging.

The Mādhyamika thus makes a distinction between the empirical, relative, mundane (saṁvṛti) and the ultimate, absolute, supramundane (paramārtha). It should be remembered of course that this is no ultimate distinction, but holds only in the realm of the empirical since no categories can apply to the ultimate. In later chapters we will discuss this exact distinction in Don Juan's discussion of the tonal and the nagual. Just as Kant regards his categories as empirically real but transcendentally ideal, so too does the Mādhyamika accept views and concepts as having phenomenal efficacy and ultimate unreality.

In order to emphasize the importance the Mādhyamika assigned to the phenomenal, Ramanan states:

> The conventional entities that constitute the mundane existence can be distinguished as of three kinds: The complex thing, the subtle constituents and the ways in which the latter combine to constitute the thing. Everyone of these has its own kind of being. Each is a kind of conventional entity with its own name. But this should not mislead one to imagine that these kinds of entities which are arrived at by logical analysis have all their own unconditional and separate existence. Of course, as relative modes of being, they not only hold good but are essential aspects of common experience.[1]

1. K. Venkata Ramanan, *Nāgārjuna's Philosophy as Presented in the Mahā-Prajñāpāramitā-Śāstra* (Bharatiya Vidya Prakashan, 1971), p. 82.

Thus Nāgārjuna does not rule out the mundane as being somehow "less real" than the ultimate. The mundane and the ultimate are two aspects of the same reality. In other words, the difference between the mundane and the ultimate (saṁvṛti and paramārtha), lies in us, and not in some supposedly "real" distinction between the two. The mundane is the real or ultimate with our own concepts superimposed upon it. The Bodhisattva erases the superimposition, but not necessarily permanently. The superimposition is used whenever pragmatically necessary, neither as a matter of habit nor compulsively as a driven man.

Throughout the history of non-Western philosophy, we find literally hundreds of "small stories." These small stories (sometimes just descriptions) are meant to slide the student from the cut and dry, analytical thinking of the dialectic into the next phase of study, namely, experience. These little stories, usually freely sprinkled with similes and metaphors, convey insight and vision beyond words. In the *Mahāprajñāpāramitā Śāstra* of Nāgārjuna, we find the explanation of the "five eyes." The reason for the introduction of the five eyes at this juncture is the conviction of the author that this particular little story captures the essence of the traversing of the path from the eyes of the flesh to the eyes of the Buddha. These five eyes represent five levels of understanding. They are:

	Sanskrit
1. The eyes of flesh	(Māṁsacakṣus)
2. The Deva eyes	(divyacakṣus)
3. The eye of wisdom	(prajñācakṣus)
4. The eye of dharma	(dharmacakṣus)
5. The eye of Buddha	(Buddhacakṣus)

The bodhisattva already has the eyes of flesh and has partially even the other four kinds of eyes. But these eyes are covered up with the dust of the limitations of sin (i.e. ignorance and passion) . . .[1]

1. K. Venkata Ramanan, *Nāgārjuna's Philosophy as Presented in the Mahā-Prajñāpāramitā-Śāstra* (Bharatiya Vidya Prakashan, 1971), p. 120.

The task of the bodhisattva is to purify all five eyes. Purification consists of not clinging to the elements of these levels of understanding.

The eyes of flesh are purified by the performance of moral deeds. We will speak of this in later chapters in the discussion of Don Juan's teaching of "sweeping the tonal clean." The eyes of flesh, as implied by the name, see only the immediate.

The deva (divine) eyes see further; they see the Karmic chain and factors of the Karmic chain such as good and bad, causal relations, etc.[1] These eyes are purified by dhyāna. Both eyes of flesh and deva eyes see in terms of poles, dualities. Through Dhyāna (meditation), and not clinging to the powers of flesh and analysis (clinging to the powers of the flesh means clinging to any object of the senses), the bodhisattva views through the eyes of wisdom. The eyes of wisdom see Nirvāna, the undifferentiated oneness, the universe through no categories. Don Juan's equivalent of this is "seeing." His remedy for clinging to the deva eye is "stopping the world." Again these will be discussed in later chapters.

> In the ultimate truth all the different views disappear, all the activities of the mind return and enter the dharmatā (Nirvāṇa) and there is no other sphere for the mind to reach. There all words cease: the world is itself beheld in its true nature as Nirvāṇa and not anything different. It is this wisdom by means of which one realizes this ultimate truth that is called the eye of wisdom.[2]

Once one has seen through the eye of wisdom, one no longer clings to the elements of analysis, whether they be "mundane", "transmundane" or "Nirvāṇa." In the Śāstra, Nāgārjuna gives us a good feeling for what is meant by the eye of wisdom with respect to the farer of the middle way.[3] He says that should the farer view only the composite (mundane), he would fall victim to the false notion of existence. If the farer views

1. K. Venkata Ramanan, *Nāgārjuna's Philosophy as Presented in the Mahā-Prajñāpāramitā-Śāstra* (Bharatiya Vidya Prakashan, 1971), p. 121.
2. ibid., p. 122.
3. ibid., p. 123.

only the incomposite (transmundane), he would fall victim to the false notion of non-existence.

> . . .Abandoning these extremes, by means of unerring wisdom, he fares the Middle Way. This is the eye of wisdom. . . Realizing the eye of wisdom, one puts an end to all elements of ignorance, general or particular, to everything that owes its being to ignorance.[1]

While the eye of wisdom is a completely personal perspective, the eye of dharma reveals its vision from the infinite compassion for all sentient beings. The eye of dharma sees the different ways in which people conceptualize. Since bodhisattva promises to save all beings, he realizes that the only way in which this can be done is by uncovering the eye of dharma and seeing into the conceptual networks of people. In this way, the bodhisattva can clearly see and define the conceptual monsters lurking in the corners and show them as being papier-mache, unreal. The monsters are concepts. They turn into papier-mache when one sees them to be relative constructs, mutually dependent poles, empty (śūnyatā). Only with the eye of dharma can a bodhisattva guide others to Nirvāṇa via distinct, individualized paths suited to their own particular set of circumstances.

When all of these eyes are completely purified, the bodhisattva cultivates the eye of Buddha. This eye is not separate from or the same as the other four. The eye of Buddha incorporates all the levels spoken of above into "a basic integration; in this eye the other eyes find their consummation."[2] In the words of Don Juan, the mark of a sorcerer is the ability to freely traverse between the world of the sorcerer and the world of men, not clinging to either. A fuller treatment of this parallel will be offered in later chapters.

In summarizing our account, we can say that the farer of the Middle way begins his path with a working knowledge of the dialectic (prasaṅga). The dialectic shows the farer that all

1. K. Venkata Ramanan, *Nāgārjuna's Philosophy as Presented in the Mahā-Prajñāpāramitā-Śāstra* (Bharatiya Vidya Prakashan, 1971), p. 123.

2. ibid., pp. 124-125.

theories of the world are built of concepts, which are mental abstractions about the world. These abstractions are empty (śūnyatā) in that any pole—hot, high, round, substance, etc.—is undefinable except in terms of its opposite—cold, low, flat, attribute.

The bodhisattva realizes that clinging to any of these elements as indicative of the real is ignorance (avidyā) and is to be avoided at all costs. The farer is then on the road to the purification of all of the levels of understanding (eyes) through meditation, dhyāna, and development of infinite compassion.

This chapter is intended to introduce the philosophy of the Mādhyamika. In no way is it anything but a capsule view. As and when needed, further elaboration, clarification as well as the introduction of other ideas will be undertaken in the treatment of the teachings of Don Juàn in the following chapters.

Chapter III

CONSCIOUSNESS: ORDINARY AND NON-ORDINARY MODES

> From the moment we become all 'tonal' we begin making pairs. We sense our two sides, but we always represent them with items of the 'tonal'. We say that the two parts of us are the soul and the body. Or mind and matter. Or good and evil. God and Satan. We never realize, however, that we are merely pairing things on the island, very much like pairing coffee and tea, or bread and tortillas, or chili and mustard. I tell you, we are weird animals. We get carried away and in our madness we believe ourselves to be making perfect sense.[1]

As we look around us in our day-to-day lives, we observe the world in what we think is all its glory. We see an object, it is tall, with bark and leaves; it is a tree. We see an animal with four legs, it barks, it is a dog. We see a geographical protrusion consisting of boulders and dirt, it is a mountain. For purposes of our thought these things are unchanging, in the sense that our definitions of the terms referring to them remain the same through time. Barring some natural catastrophe, our definition of "Mount Whitney" is the same today as it was yesterday. Occasionally we are jolted by some philosopher like Heraclitus who tells us that we can never step into the same river twice and we are reminded that there is change in the world. The mountain washes to the sea, and the dog dies.

This is no revelation. Our world is a jumping back and forth between substance and process. Some claim that ultimate

1. Carlos Castaneda, *Tales of Power* (New York: Simon and Schuster, 1974), p. 123.

reality is of the nature of substance, while others claim that it is process. In the present chapter, we will argue that since substance and process are two mutually dependent categories (as shown in chapter two), they are not indicative of the real. This is not to say that these concepts are totally useless. They are necessary in our daily lives. Our working, living and eating take place as a result of communication with others, a communication whose life breath is these dichotomies. Dichotomies are at the heart of language and conceptual thinking: but does this mean that reality is also constituted of dichotomies ?

The world is not a still frame out of a motion picture. It is not even the motion picture. This is not to say that the world is a continual stream either, but since scientists tell us that there is motion in everything and everywhere, and since as much as we hate to admit it, everything erodes and changes, let us for the moment think of the world as a stream. By the way, by "world" here, we are referring to all that we can experience through our perceptual-conceptual mechanisms. If we think of the world in this way, our thoughts might proceed as follows. The sun feeds energy to the plants and other creatures. Plants and animals breathe out complementary mixtures. That is, plants exhale oxygen while animals inhale oxygen. Similarly, the animals exhale carbon dioxide while plants inhale the same. Plants and animals grow and die. They are either eaten or simply decay. If they are eaten, they are immediately assimilated into the living and growing of other creatures. If they decay, they compose the earth out of which plants grow, and life in general erupts. Whatever the creature does not immediately need of what it has eaten is eliminated and enters the soil. From this apparent "waste" as well as from the eroding of mountains and other phenomena, minerals are deposited into the ground which contribute toward future plants. When we combine with this the reproductive mechanisms of all living things, we visualize a stream where none of these entities of which we have spoken is an individual. The tree breathes in the mixture which I breathe out. I breathe in the mixture which the tree breathes out. I eat the fruit of the tree. The fruit is a product of the minerals and the sun and innumerable other factors. My body transmutes the fruit into energy which makes me grow. I eliminate whatever is immediately unuseful, and it enters the soil cycle and is transferred into minerals and other things. The world flows each day in just this way only billionfold more complex.

When we view the world in such a way, entities lose their independence. No longer do we think of that tall oak tree as an independent entity. It is just as dependent on us as we on it. The tree and we are just as dependent on other things in the world as they are on us.

Where, then, is there substance in the world ? It is nowhere to be found when we look at the world in the manner described above. We are not hereby saying that the world is a process, pure and simple. After all, conceptually, process and substance are mutually dependent categories, just as phenomenologically we and all other entities in the world are mutually dependent. To think of process without substance is as impossible as the tree without the sun. This is the principle of dependent origination as referred to by the Buddhists. This is also the teaching of Don Juan.

Upon Castaneda's first visits to Don Juan, the latter suggested that he talk to plants and animals, to consider them as equals, but Castaneda only considered it ludicrous. To apologize to a plant for taking its life was to Castaneda absurd. Later, however, it became not so absurd:

> I looked down at the ground and caught sight of a large black beetle. It came out from behind a small rock, pushing a ball of dung twice its size. I followed its movements for a long time. The insect seemed unconcerned with my presence and kept on pushing its load over rocks, roots, depressions and protruberences on the ground. For all I knew, the beetle was not aware that I was there. The thought occurred to me that I could not possibly be sure that the insect was not aware of me: that thought triggered a series of rational evaluations about the nature of the insect's world as opposed to mine. The beetle and I were in the same world and obviously the world was not the same for both of us . . .
>
> I observed the insect for a long time and then I became aware of the silence around me. Only the wind hissed

> between the branches and leaves of the chaparral. I looked up, turned to my left in a quick and involuntary fashion, and caught a glimpse of a faint shadow or flicker on a rock a few feet away. At first I paid no attention to it but then I realized that that flicker had been to my left. I turned again suddenly and was able to clearly perceive a shadow on the rock. I had a weird sensation that the shadow instantly slid down to the ground and the soil absorbed it as a blotter dries an ink blotch. A chill ran down my back. The thought crossed my mind that death was watching me and the beetle. . . .
>
> The beetle emerged from a deep hole and stopped a few inches from my face. It seemed to look at me and for a moment I felt that it became aware of my presence, perhaps as I was aware of the presence of my death. I experienced a shiver. The beetle and I were not that different after all. Death, like a shadow, was stalking both of us from behind the boulder. I had an extraordinary moment of elation. The beetle and I were on a par. Neither of us was better than the other. Our death made us equal.[1]

At this point Castaneda had a loss of ego. He did not consider himself to be better than a common beetle. This loss of ego triggered in him a vision of the world that cannot be considered ordinary. His ally appeared, a coyote. Castaneda had a conversation with the coyote. After this,

> The coyote stood up and our eyes met. I felt that they were pulling me and suddenly the animal became iridescent; it began to glow. It was as if my mind were replaying the memory of another event that had taken place ten years before, when under the influence of peyote I witnessed the metamorphosis of an ordinary dog into an unforgettable iridescent being. It was as though the coyote had triggered the recollection, and the memory of that previous event was summoned and became superimposed on the coyote's shape; the coyote was a fluid liquid, luminous being . . .

1. Carlos Castaneda, *Journey to Ixtlan* (New York: Simon and Schuster, 1972), pp. 248-49.

> The luminous being touched me in some unidentified part of myself and my body experienced such an exquisite indescribable warmth and well-being that it was as if the touch had made me explode. I became transfixed. I could not feel my feet, or my legs, or any part of my body, yet something was sustaining me erect.
>
> I have no idea how long I stayed in that position. In the meantime, the luminous coyote and the hilltop where I stood melted away. I had no thoughts or feelings. Everything had been turned off and I was floating freely.[1]
>
> I stayed on the hilltop in a state of ecstasy for what appeared to be an endless time, yet the whole event may have lasted for only a few minutes, perhaps only as long as the sun shone before it reached the horizon, but to me it seemed an endless time. I felt something warm and soothing oozing out of the world and out of my own body. I knew I had discovered a secret. It was so simple. I experienced an unknown flood of feeling. Never in my life had I had such a divine euphoria, such peace, such an encompassing grasp, and yet I could not put the discovered secret into words, or even into thoughts, but my body knew it.[2]

The above is referred to by Don Juan as "stopping the world." It is the same as the Buddhist's Nirvāṇa. We find a similar description of the above experience in Herbert Guenther's *The Life and Teachings of Naropa*. Naropa was a Tibetan saint who lived almost 1,000 years ago and was the student of Tilopa.

> 'Remove all evil and purify me from it.' When properly practiced it is as if both deities, rDorje sems-dpa and rDo-rje snems-ma, were saying; 'All your evil has been purified.' At this moment the deities and oneself dissolve in an experience of ineffable light, and one may remain in this state of utter composure as long as one likes. This is the 'Ultimate rDo-rje sems-dpa,' the experience of the Real

1. Carlos Castaneda, *Journey to Ixtlan* (New York: Simon and Schuster, 1972), pp. 251-52.
2. ibid., pp. 252-53.

as such. It is also named Jñānavajrayoga (ye-ses rdo-rje rnal-'byor), living up to transcending awareness as the ground of our whole being.[1]

The reason for these long quotes is that we wish to exhibit the links of the chain between seeing the world as substance or seeing it as process, and then upon the principle of mutual dependence, seeing the world as neither substance nor process nor any combination of these two or other dichotomies. The link seems to be this: when we look at the world as made up of substances, we are individuals, opposed to one another. When we see it as process, we realize that things are not so discreet, via the principle of dependent origination[2] (Pratītyasamutpāda). When we eliminate the ego we can see the world without the barriers that language and thought impose. As Castaneda said, the experience cannot be verbalized. To verbalize in this case is to indulge in a reductionism ending in our speaking of a still frame of experience and thus losing the experience itself.

What, then, is the difference between non-ordinary reality and ordinary reality ? Put briefly, ordinary reality is the world experienced through our senses and language of everyday life. Non-ordinary reality is experienced only when we "stop the world," that is only when we experience the world without the encumbrance of perceptual-conceptual frameworks.

According to Nāgārjuna, "substance" and "process" are concepts which in themselves are empty (śūnyatā). That is to say that these concepts as well as all other concepts and conceptual networks, however complex, derive their meanings not from the world itself but from their opposite and mutually dependent categories. While we cannot and need not examine all categories and categoric frameworks with the eye of Nāgārjuna's prasaṅga, suffice it to note that thinking is always through some form or other, and our everyday lives are filled with only these thought forms. According to Don Juan, in order

1. Herbert V. Guenther, *The Life and Teaching of Naropa* (London: Oxford University Press, 1963), p. 133.

2. K. Venkata Ramanan, *Nāgārjuna's Philosophy as Presented in the Mahā-Prajñāpāramitā-Śāstra* (Bharatiya Vidya Prakashan, 1971), pp. 138, 160, 165-68.

to experience non-ordinary reality, one has to shut off the internal dialogue, namely, the incessant chattering of thought forms in our minds.

> 'Seeing' happens only when the warrior is capable of stopping the internal dialogue.
>
> Today you stopped your talk at will, out there in the bushes. And you 'saw.' What you saw was not clear. You thought that it was a man. I say it was a moth. Neither of us is correct, but that's because we have to talk.[1]

What happens when one 'stops the world'? All we can say is that one experiences the world without the veil of the usual armor of name (concept) and form (percept). Castaneda was able to record his feelings and perceptions, but he too finally admits that the experience eludes all description.

To shed light on the subject, Don Juan alludes to the emptiness of words when Castaneda says that a certain explanation is not good enough.

> 'That's the flaw with words,' he said in an assuring tone. 'They always force us to feel enlightened, but when we turn around to face the world they always fail us and we end up facing the world as we always have, without enlightenment. For this reason a sorcerer seeks to act rather than to talk and to this effect he gets a new description of the world—a new description where talking is not that important, and where new acts have new reflections.'[2]

In order to further clarify the point, Don Juan introduces the notions 'tonal' and 'nagual.'[3] He explains that all human beings have these two aspects, the tonal and the nagual. The tonal is the "social person," "the organizer of the world," "a protector." This protector or guardian who is "broad minded and understanding" becomes "narrow minded and despotic."[4]

1. Carlos Castaneda, *Tales of Power* (New York: Simon and Schuster, 1974), p. 34.
2. ibid., p. 32.
3. ibid., p. 121.
4. ibid., pp. 122-23.

Put simply, the tonal is our description of the world: "It can be said that the tonal is everything that meets the eye."[1] The tonal begins at birth and ends at death. Don Juan later states that the tonal makes the world in that it creates the world by interpreting it within its own rules. Thus our world is the tonal. Included within that tonal is every concept, every God, heaven, good, etc.—in short, everything that can be sensed and thought.

The Madhyamaka equivalent for the tonal is the saṁvṛti (the mundane). Within the saṁvṛti lie all dualisms, including that of saṁvṛti and paramārtha (the Madhyamaka equivalent of nagual). It may be noted in passing that the Advaita Vedānta equivalent of this dualism is saguṇa and nirguṇa Brahman. Saguṇa Brahman is reality as grasped through names and forms; and Nirguṇa Brahman is reality beyond names and forms.

If tonal (saṁvṛti) is all that we can speak of, then what is the nagual (paramārtha)? The nagual is that state of consciousness which the internal dialogue has ceased; as such, it is the consciousness in which "seeing" takes place. Talk of "seeing" pervades Castaneda's four volumes. We will here try to give the gist of what is meant by it, and illustrate the point from the lives of one of Tibet's saints.

Don Juan states that to look at a man is to look at the features of his tonal, but to "see" a man is to see him not as arms, trunk, and legs, but to view him as luminous fibers forming a luminous egg.[2] The luminous is only a description in terms of the tonal, and thereby merely a pointer toward an extraordinary experience and reality.

These sorts of descriptions are extremely limited, and would be totally alien to us were it not for some of the scant literature coming from Tibet and a few other places. In fact, an exact description of the luminous egg can be found in the *Hundred Thousand Songs of Milarepa.* At the end of Marpa's (Milarepa's guru) life, Milarepa journeyed a great distance for the funeral. Upon his return, he found at the cremation house people

1. Carlos Castaneda, *Tales of Power* (New York: Simon and Schuster. 1974), pp. 98-99.
2. Carlos Castaneda, *A Separate Reality* (New York: Simon and Schuster, 1971), pp. 23, 153, 159.

gathered around phenomena of varying account. Some saw "Dorje's," others saw balls of light, some saw a pool of water.[1] This is reminiscent of Don Juan's display of power when he looked like a pirate to one, a rich gentleman to another, and a beggar to another.[2]

As Milarepa's song of his guru's death goes on, we hear that the dakinis (goddesses who have occult powers) had come to take Marpa away. Marpa's students were clamoring for a relic of Marpa, as an object of devotion and power. Those gathered had sung a song and,

> When they had sung this mournful prayer, there descended from the sphere of light, which was in the hands of the Dakinis, *a lustrous relique like an orb as large as an egg.* In a streak of light it came down directly upon the funeral pyre. All the disciples stretched out their hands eagerly, each claiming it for himself. But the relique went back again to the fermament, and was absorbed in the sphere of light which the Dakinis still held in their hands.[3]

When this happened, the two Dakinis who were guarding the "chaitya" bearing Marpa came down and sang a song. In this song, the Dakinis describe how the power of their prayers had brought a relic, the luminous egg. An object, even if merely seen, could save beings from the interminable rounds of birth and death. An object

> . . . which, if believed in, bringeth Buddhahood. The Dharma-Kâya—a single sphere its symbol—brought forth, to be that relique, *which is egg-shaped* . . .[4]

The poem goes on to describe how the orb is all of ours and yet none of ours to cling to, and hence was retracted into the

1. W.Y. Evans-Wentz, *Tibet's Great Yogi Milarepa* (2d ed. London: Oxford University Press, 1951), p. 289.

2. Carlos Castaneda, *Journey to Ixtlan* (New York: Simon and Schuster, 1972), p. 207 ff.

3. W.Y. Evans-Wentz, *Tibet's Great Yogi Milarepa* (2d ed. London: Oxford University Press, 1951), p. 291 (emphasis added).

4. ibid., p.292 (emphasis added).

heavens. After this, the song exhorts us to discriminate between true wisdom and delusion:

> The serving of a perfect Guru,
> And the serving of a person of
>   good fortune,
> Appear to be alike, but beware,
>   and confuse them not.
>
> The true dawning of the voidness
>   in one's mind,
> And illusory obsessions of the
>   consciousness,
> Appear to be alike, but beware,
>   and confuse them not . . .[1]

The song goes on to praise the glory of the paramārtha (nagual), and then tells of the states of the saṁvṛti (tonal) that drive us to cling to them. Thus in the second stanza the distinction is drawn between the state of emptiness achieved by exercise, and the flooded confused state of mind that the majority of us are in our entire lives. In the eleventh stanza of this part of the song, we once again find the orb mentioned:

> The Orb of Dharma-Kāya, (blemishless),
> And the relic orb formed of earthly
>   matter,
> Appear alike, but beware,
>   and confuse them not.[2]

It is worth noting that the relic orb referred to here is the orb which came from Marpa on a thread of light. This is the relic orb referred to in this stanza as the one not to be confused with the real orb, that of the Dharma-Kāya. The Dharma-Kāya is the Body of Truth, it is qualityless.[3] It seems then that what

---

1. W.Y. Evans-Wentz, *Tibet's Great Yogi Milarepa* (2d ed. London: Oxford University Press, 1951), p. 299.
2. ibid.
3. ibid., pp. 37-38.

Marpa is saying in his final message is that on the path to world-transcending Buddhahood, the truth (if it can still be called anything at all) is revealed to us in the form of a luminous egg. Since the description of the luminous egg lies completely within the realm of the saṁsāra (the mundane), this description certainly belongs in the tonal. However, it can serve as a pointer to an experience beyond the realm of names and forms (nāma and rūpa).

This is exactly what Don Juan has to say of the subject. Even though both Don Juan's and Milarepa's descriptions are couched in their own language and social history, those of the Tibetan yogis and those of American Indian warriors and sorcerers, one thing is clear. That is, their basic insights are the same. There is a part of us which lives in the world of names and forms. For most of us, this part is all we know. But there is another part, a part known to only a few, the enlightened. In this world, polar knowledge is useless, and only the firsthand, unmediated experience is present. The tonal and the nagual, or the saṁsāra and Nirvāṇa are two parts of all beings. Ultimately, however, there is no difference between the two, but this will be discussed later. In this world, nameless and formless, the luminous egg is but one portion. It is common to the Tibetans and Don Juan.

. . . . . .

To us, locked in our everyday lives, this talk of tonal and nagual, saṁvṛti and paramārtha seems too distant indeed. When do we experience the dakinis and sages of Tibet ? Or the allies and sorcerers of Don Juan ? To us who never think of our own consciousness as cluttered with useless and even detrimental ramblings, the world is square and angular, cut and dry, black and white (some of our intellectuals even allowing a little gray). What, then, makes us think that the world might be different than everyone says it is ? How does the tonal immersed man even suspect this "other"?

These thoughts come to us in various ways. One way is to inspect the universe with the very tools that we have, and at the same time we can investigate the tools themselves. We must be careful not to fall into the mundane habit of inspecting the tools for mere efficiency. Our scientists do a good job of this. Our interest is in the tools themselves. We must investigate the nature of these tools at least insofar as they bear upon our discussion of non-ordinary reality.

One tool which plays a central role in our investigation of the world is mathematics. There are certainly other tools e.g., language, as discussed in chapter 2, with which we arm ourselves in our undertaking of "making sense of the world," but mathematics is a far-reaching topic, its impact being constantly visible in our everyday world. It is to a discussion of this karmic magnitude of mathematics that we shall now turn.

When a man on the street wonders at the marvels of science and technology, he might think of mathematicians and scientists as having the world by the tail. "Sure, they might not know everything, but with all of their knowledge they certainly have the tools in their hands to know everything that is important. Just look at the miracle of T.V." This might seem to be the case, for, after all, these men have the facility to think in terms of mind-boggling equations as mysterious to the layman as the great pyramids. These are the men who play with formulas, cure diseases, enhance productivity, and in general make our lives easier. Thus it is understandable if one thinks that the only way to enhance ourselves is to follow the path of science and technology that we have, hoping that someday they will lead us to some ultimate panacea.

It should be stated now, in order to ward off any misunderstanding, that we do not mean to belittle such enterprise. All that we wish to point out is that the above view is misleading. Let us investigate exactly what these enterprises entail.

When there is an event in the world that we are interested in, we load up our necessary theoretical gear, physical law, mathematics, etc. In some way or other, we must isolate this event, since our theories and mathematics are of an ideal nature. We find which aspects of the phenomena are relevant and apply our theoretical frameworks to it. When we speak of a body in motion we think of two things, the body itself and the point of reference (or the observer). We are saying that these two are things, but they are actually treated as non-things, i.e. the body is a point mass, the observer is the base of the coordinate system. What we are saying here is that it is the nature of mathematical and scientific enterprise to give us a reductionistic view of the world. Not even a view of the world, but of only a minute corner of it.

Let us take an example of one of the most simple physical processes, the motion of a ball. We view the motion of a thrown ball as ruled by Newton's second law of motion, F=ma, with the force being generated in accordance with the law of gravitation. This is usually as far as the matter goes since all that we normally care to know is how far the ball will go and how long it will take. However, just as a thought experiment, let us pursue further. These most simple physical equations grow enormously when we remove them from their simplistic contexts. Thus let us see the ball from a broader and hence less reductionistic matrix. The ball begins to take on a past, present and future. It has a complexion, it evolved from a rubber tree somewhere which produced a sticky substance of enormous chemical complexity by interacting with its constantly changing surroundings in countless ways. The tree takes the sunlight, minerals, soil, water, its own genetic structure all leading to its famous product, namely, rubber. This rubber then follows a complicated path through refineries and trucks and then to the store shelf and then on to you, who bounce it into the air taking a few measurements and then on. Its history goes to the point of its disintegration which is actually not a point, but a period of lapsed time (it is a point only for our convenience). At its time of disintegration its billions of molecules disperse in a million directions. We can see that any sort of mathematical description of the total biography of the ball is out of the question. The equations are too enormous to comprehend, because the situation itself is too complex.

The matter is further complicated were we to include the surroundings or environment of the ball. After all, in the ball's life, however short, it has had millions of subvisual interactions and many visual ones. Einstein gives us a glimmer of further complications by adding hitherto unsuspected dimensions to the Newtonian theory. But when we take a phenomenon out of its isolated, reduced state of study, the phenomenon goes from being a bare skeleton, point mass describing a simple arc, to a phenomenon so complex that mathematics finds itself incapable of even facing the task of description. We can neither experience nor know the world at large by looking at it through equations and scientific theory.

We do not mean to sell these endeavors short, relegating them to the realm of the false and useless. These things certainly have pragmatic value. On the other hand, we must struggle against the constant temptation to think of things in the universe as point masses, disconnected from everything else and eagerly waiting to be drawn into our mathematical-theoretical networks. The things of the world, even the most simple, are unboundedly complex in their relationship to other things. Our mathematics and science, while well meant, mislead us into thinking that the world is made up of events so simple as to be represented by equations. The most complex mathematical equations are infinitely simple compared to the complexity of something like the leaf in the life-cycle of a tree, or the life of the insignificant fly. And if these small (!) things are infinitely complex, then their matrix, namely, the world, is infinitely more so. We marvel at page-long equations, but it rarely occurs to us that the thoughts which pass through our minds in a split flash are much more complex in logic (form).

Is mathematics or science useless then ? Certainly not. Quite the contrary. We must, however, remember that a science or a study, by its very nature is not a study of the world but of the *skeleton* of some submicroscopic element of that world, and an idealized view at that. Forgetting this, we find ourselves in ordinary reality, as we are everyday.

But what happens if we do think of the world in this way? Let us think of the consequences. To begin with, the identities of things change. The robin in the tree is no longer the point mass at the center of some imaginary target in the sights of our indiscriminate B-B gun, but a nice collection of sights and sounds infinitely complex, infinitely mysterious. The insect is no more a black spot on the periphery of our vision whose only place in the world is under the shoe, but an interesting collection of energy which fearlessly enters the life-cycle of yet another being. In short these "things" in our world become alive, and in doing so lose their photograph like boundaries and melt with their surroundings which have also lost their concrete distinctness. Is it absurd, then, to suggest that we too eventually lose our distinction when we realize that we and our environment are also one breathing organism ? As Castaneda realized, he and the beetle had something in common after all.

To dramatize their conversation to this effect, Don Juan reminded Castaneda of a story that Carlos had told him. Previously, Castaneda had remarked that he and a friend had observed that when a leaf fell from a tree, it was an event never to be repeated in an infinity of time.[1] When Castaneda agreed that this is still what he thought to be the case, Don Juan took him to a place where there was a tall tree. He instructed Castaneda to watch a leaf fall from the tree.

> "Did you see it ?"
> "Yes."
> "You would say that the same leaf will
> never again fall from the same tree,
> true?"
> "True."
>
> "From the best of your understanding that is true. But that is only to the best of your understanding. Look again."
>
> "I automatically looked and saw a leaf falling. It actually hit the same leaves and branches as the previous one. It was as if I were looking at an instant television replay. I followed the wavy falling of the leaf until it landed on the ground. I stood up to find out if there were two leaves, but the tall underbrush around the tree prevented me from seeing where the leaf had actually landed."
>
> "Don Juan laughed and told me to sit down."
>
> " 'Look,' he said, pointing with his head to the top of the tree. 'There goes the same leaf again.' "
>
> "I once more saw a leaf falling in exactly the same pattern as the previous two . . ."[2]

---

1. Carlos Castaneda, *A Separate Reality* (New York: Simon and Schuster, 1971), p. 259.
2. ibid., pp. 259-60.

The pattern was again and again repeated. Castaneda continues:

> "He laughed but did not answer and I insisted that he should tell me how I could see that leaf falling over and over. I said that according to my reason that was impossible . . .
>
> 'You're chained!' Don Juan exclaimed. 'You're chained to your reason.'
>
> "He explained that the leaf had fallen over and over from the same tree so I would stop trying to understand . . .
>
> 'There's nothing to understand. Understanding is only a very small affair, so very small,' he said."[1]

Clearly, Don Juan's implication is that the non-ordinary reality of which he speaks is to be found, not by devising further and more elaborate cerebral feats, but in the exact opposite. That is, through practice, one transcends the boundaries of categories, logic and mathematics to the experience of the world directly. And since Castaneda's apprenticeship spanned at least 15 years (possibly to this present date) we can tell that this is not an overnight affair. It is an extremely difficult path :

> The sphere of the speakable is the domain of the determinate; the sphere where the words do not reach is the highest dharma.[2]

---

1. Carlos Castaneda, *A Separate Reality* (New York: Simon and Schuster, 1971), p. 260.

2. K. Venkata Ramanan, *Nagarjuna's Philosophy as Presented in the Maha-Prajnaparamita-Sastra* (Bharatiya Vidya Prakashan, 1971), p. 141.

CHAPTER IV

LANGUAGE AND REALITY IN DON JUAN

> "Today all I could 'see' was the movement of the 'nagual' gliding through the trees and whirling around us. Anyone who 'sees' can witness that."
>
> "What about someone who doesn't 'see' ?
>
> "He would witness nothing, just the trees being blown by a wild wind perhaps. We interpret any unknown expression of the 'nagual' as something we know; in this case the 'nagual' might be interpreted as a breeze shaking the leaves, or even as some strange light, perhaps a lightning bug of unusual size. If a man who doesn't 'see' is pressed, he would say that he thought he saw something but could not remember what. This is only natural. The man would be talking sense. After all, his eyes would have judged nothing extraordinary; being the eyes of the 'tonal' they have to be limited to the 'tonal's' world, and in that world, there is nothing staggeringly new, nothing which the eyes cannot apprehend and the 'tonal' cannot explain."[1]

Language and reality, in that combination, have at once fascinated and plagued philosophers through centuries. I say "in that combination" because either topic in isolation, while vast and interesting, would not bear the dialectical fruit needed for our present discussion as it concerns the teachings of Don Juan. The philosophical problem concerns the relation between language and reality. What is the nature of this relation ? Predictably, the narrow scope of language ties a philosopher

1. Carlos Castaneda, *Tales of Power* (New York: Simon and Schuster, 1974), pp. 190-91.

to one side or the other of the relationship, and sight is lost of the organic whole and hence their mutual dependence (pratītya-samutpāda). Concretely, the philosopher becomes either a realist, in the sense that language mirrors the world, or an idealist, in the sense that language produces the world. Also possible are various combinations of idealism and realism. These lead to even more complex problems, as will be seen presently. Nonetheless all arguments take one or the other of the four forms of the dialectic as discussed in chapter 2. As a result, any positive statement about ultimate reality can be shown to be self-contradictory.

In general, what philosophers do is to investigate the problem of the relation between language and reality with language being an integral element of the relation itself. When we explicate reality in terms of language, we beg the question as to whether or not language tinges reality or makes it or merely describes it. I say that it begs these questions, because ultimately these are the questions to which philosophers come. "What is the nature of the real?" "Is it created by language?" Or "Does it exist objectively?" In search of answers to these questions, philosophy over the ages has piloted us on a flight over such dangerous landscapes as substance, process, mind, body, cause, effect, a priori, a posteriori, and more!

Have we solved these problems? Not at all. We are stranded on a subway network produced by language, not even realizing that there is fresh air and sunshine above to be enjoyed, if we can only cease to cling to our network of language. Of course we must talk about this "letting go," so we are not referring to a total abandonment. Rather, we wish to bring some of the concepts developed by Don Juan as well as Nāgārjuna to bear upon these questions.

Recall in chapter 2, in the explication of the Madhyamaka dialectic, it was shown that in general concepts are mutually dependent (pratītya-samutpāda). Such is the nature of cause and effect, substance and process, etc. Such also is the nature of language and thought. Attribute is empirical, while substance is not; and although one can and does sensibly talk of causes and effects in the empirical world, one cannot talk of the first cause, which is certainly non-empirical. Language is empirical, thought is not. Yet somehow these poles are locked together. This magnetism is what has enchanted philosophy. Unfortunately, in their zealousness to defend some ontology or other, philosophers have failed to recognize the organic nature of language and thought.

Adam Schaff is a modern Marxist who discusses the problem and purportedly comes to a resolution.[1] And to some extent Schaff *does recognize* the organic unity of language and thought. Schaff even explicates a larger organism where society, language and thought are intimately related.

While Schaff quite readily admits that language has a built-in Weltanschaung, he even goes so far as to suggest a modified picture theory of knowledge. According to the picture theory, language and thought mirror the world. Schaff suggests that there is an objective reality which, when observed by a person, presents itself with an interpretation imposed on it by the language-thought system of that person.[2] In addition, man's language is shaped by his "social-practical activity."[3] According to Schaff,

> Language is in that sense a kind of condensed practical activity, which affects our actual process of cognition in the most suggestive and easiest way.
>
> First of all, language affects the way we perceive reality. We now have experimental data to support the thesis that our perception of reality is clearly affected by the language in which we think. This only means that language, which is a kind of copy of reality, is also a kind of maker of our image of reality.[4]

This is not to say that Schaff is saying that reality is totally subjective; quite the contrary Schaff continues:

> Depending on their environment, men may formulate the same meanings in different ways; may experience them in

---

1. Adam Schaff, *Language and Cognition*, trans. Olgierd Wojtasiewicz (New York: McGraw-Hill, Inc., 1973).
2. ibid., pp. 123, 137, 144-45.
3. ibid., p. 137.
4. ibid., pp. 145-46.

> the form of different images, may focus their attention on different things and phenomena, depending on the conditions imposed upon them by their struggle for existence; and may classify fragments of objective reality in different ways. But their image of reality is in general the same. . .[1]

Schaff's defense of this thesis is two-fold. First, since languages are mutually translatable,[2] all men conceptualize the same things, with differences occurring only as minor quirks. We should note here that millions of lives have been lost in wars, police actions, and local disputes as a result of these quirks. I can only suggest that they are not small and irrelevant but rather large and significant quirks.

Earlier in this same book, Schaff refers to the Hopi Indian language as having the concept of space in common with ours, but lacking our concept of time. Surely a conceptual network not employing our concept of time is not translatable into our language. The world portrayed by the Hopi language is not the world portrayed by the English language. This does not mean in any way that the Hopi language creates a less accurate picture of the world. It is a legitimate language that visualizes the world in a radically different way from ours.

As for the second defense, Schaff says that all men have a common biological basis, i.e. neuro-physiological makeup. In this way, people can travel from one continent to another, learn other languages and communicate. This is what makes possible the translatability of all languages.

While we certainly agree that all men have roughly the same neuro-physiological makeup, this does not prove that there is an objective reality totally different from our perceptual networks, and that this objective reality is roughly the same for all individuals in all languages.

Discussing the translation of Hungarian and Frisian into English, W.V.O. Quine writes:

---

1. Adam Schaff, *Language and Cognition*, trans. Olgierd Wojtasiewicz (New York: McGraw-Hill, Inc., 1973), pp. 148-49.

2. ibid., p. 148.

> It would be trivial to say that we cannot know the meaning of a foreign sentence except as we are prepared to offer a translation in our own language. I am saying more: that it is only relative to an, in large part, arbitrary manual of translation that most foreign sentences may be said to share the same meaning of English sentences, and then only in a very parochial sense of meaning, viz., use in English.[1]

It is not the intent of this chapter to criticize Schaff or to defend Quine. What is hoped is that in this brief space we can give some feeling of the dialectical matrix in which the language-reality dichotomy resides. Schaff's deduction follows the same route as all transcendental deductions, i.e. all arguments which try to establish ties between the empirical and the non-empirical. [It should be noted here that the mutual dependence of concepts is a relation between linguistic entities (concepts) and not between linguistic and extralinguist c entities.] That is, on the basis of empirical evidence, namely the biological argument and the translatability argument, Schaff tries to establish that there is an objective reality and that it appears to all men in basically the same form. Schaff takes what he thinks is a middle position between extreme realism and extreme idealism, accepting from both some aspects, and rejecting others. This is the spirit of the Marxian dialectic. Also, in the nature of the Marxian dialectic, Schaff introduces a third concept that is on a plateau above the first two. This is where trouble begins.

According to prasaṅga, *any* theoretical construction *when considered as an absolute* statement about the world, leads inevitably to self contradiction. While steering clear of the pitfalls of the first two categories of Nāgārjuna's dialectic, (i.e. in this case idealism and realism) Schaff falls victim to the third category (i.e. any amalgam of idealism and realism).

The contradiction in Schaff's position is this : if form lies outside of language, what possibly could be meant by 'form'?

---

1. W.V.O. Quine, "Meaning and Translation," *The Structure of Language*, ed. Jerry A. Fodor and Jerrold J. Katz (Englewood Cliffs: Prentice-Hall, Inc., 1964), p. 477.

Schaff himself says that not only everything that is spoken is thought, but everything that is thought is done so in terms of some language or other.[1] He treats this statement as synthetic, and not universally accepted, but "strongly supported by scientific data."[2] If everything that is thought is done so in terms of some language or other, then how can one even think of form apart from language? How can we know it? Scientific data can tell us nothing of it, and that is just the point.

Schaff does not help his case by saying that part of form lies in language and part in the world. It only makes us wonder what form it is that these two have in common.

Schaff certainly generates illuminating discussion in talking of the mutual dependence of thought and language as well as the mutual dependence of thought-language and society. But this is as far as analysis will allow. Language and thought will take us only to the extent of our phenomenal existence. The strongest statement that can be made then is that form lies within the realm of language. And since language (including Schaff's thought-language) lies within the realm of form (i.e. language is structured in some form or other), the two sets are identical.

What, then, is the world like apart from this psycho-linguistic grouping? The simple answer is: nothing that can be explicated in terms of this grouping.

Can we then not experience anything which is not inside the realm of our language (form)? Considering the Buddhist writings to which we referred and Castaneda's writings, our answer will be: yes, we can. Of course, this would be a 'mystic' interpretation which Schaff rejects summarily,[3] never realizing that with his inseparability of language and thought[4] comes an identity of thought and form. If form is identical with thought, then our

1. Adam Schaff, *Language and Cognition*, trans. Olgierd Wojtasiewicz (New York: McGraw-Hill, Inc., 1973), pp. 82-83.
2. ibid., p. 83.
3. ibid., p. 144.
4. ibid., p. 129.

descriptions of the world that we experience are strictly our thought, no more and no less. This leaves the 'real' in a rather dubious status. This is too much for the Marxist to bear. Language and thought only yield relative truths, that is, relative with respect to the categorical framework of a given thinker in question. We may consider as true a mathematical statement such as $V = \frac{dx}{dt}$. But to the Hopi Indian this might not be the case, not because his language is too primitive to understand derivatives, but because his conception of time is quite different from ours. Any conceptual entity, by which he replaces time is truth-bearing only within his own framework. So an outsider who feels that the Hopi's conception is naive, or patently false, cannot claim so, because the Hopi's conception (and the critic's as well) of time is only relatively true to begin with. Relative truth in this case means that the Hopi's time conception is valid for the Hopi in his own conceptual framework. Were we to remove this conception of time from its conceptual matrix and transplant it, say, into our own, the concept would develop "loose ends." This is simply to say that in the Hopi's conceptual network, his concept of time fits well (no concept can fail to engender contradictions if taken as absolute). This is like the patient who dies upon transplant, for the patient, i.e. the language recipient, is not geared (conceptually) to function concurrently within a framework whose conceptual network language is shaped around and functions dependently upon linear time, T_1.

These "loose ends" mean that the concept of time T_2 (Hopi time) cannot make connections with other concepts according to which "time marches on" (T_1).

The Hopi conception is internally consistent within the Hopi system (i.e. relatively true) but externally incorrigible[1] with respect to other systems, and vice versa. This means that the best that we can hope for are relative truths, with respect to a particular categorial framework.

1. Stephen Korner, *Categorial Frameworks* (New York: Barnes and Noble, Inc., 1970), p. 14 ff.

$$V_1 = \frac{dx}{dt_1} \quad (1) \qquad\qquad V_2 = \frac{dx}{dt_2} \quad (2)$$

(where V is velocity, x is space, and t is time.)

The x's are the same in both equations as Schaff reminds us that the spatial considerations of the Hopi are roughly the same as ours. However, we cannot say that

$$V_1 = \frac{dx}{dt_2} \quad (3)$$

We are not hereby suggesting that equation (2) is a mathematical truth for the Hopi. Rather, the point is that since in equation (2) velocity is ***conceptually different*** from that in equation (1), although x has the same meaning in both. But even if (2) were a correct statement of Hopi calculus, any form of equation (3) is still impossible. The reason for this is that if we integrate equations (1) and (2) we obtain

$$\underline{A^1} \qquad\qquad \underline{B^1}$$

$$x = \int_1 V_1 \; dt_1 \qquad\qquad x = \int_2 V_2 \; dt_2$$

resulting in, $\int_1 V_1 \, dt_1 = \int_2 V_2 dt_2$, and since $V_1 \neq V_2$, the only alternative would be that the process of integration itself must be different in the two cases. In other words, even with x remaining the same, the notion of integration must be radically different. The final breakdown results when we try to integrate across equation (3). Should we integrate with respect to t_1 or t_2? In either case the results are disastrous.

$$\underline{C^1} \qquad\qquad \underline{C^{11}}$$

$$\int_1 V_1 dt_1 = \int \frac{dx \; dt_1}{dt_2} \qquad\qquad \int_2 V_1 dt_2 = \int \frac{dx \; dt_2}{dt_1}$$

The crudity of this entire example is testimony to what happens when we try to press one conceptual scheme onto another. We wind up projecting the form of our language over that of another. This can only lead us astray. Trying to make sense of the results of our equations is like pressing the jello mold of a kangaroo over that of a donkey, hoping that the resultant amorphous torso of the donkeroo will tell us something about the real nature of these animals. This is not our only problem. We have yet to account for the dismembered sections of the jello donkey. After all, certainly his head, feet, and tail are as real as the rest of him.

No view of the world can be absolutely true, but only within its own context. What does this mean? It means that there is no overall truth with a capital T which is somehow or other outside language. Truth is an indication that a certain linguistic enterprise is in a certain configuration (form). To move from this observation to the conclusion that the world has this configuration is a step that we cannot take—*not* because we cannot experience the real (tathatā, svabhāva-śūnya dharma), but because our language cannot touch the real. We do not have to deny that language is a manifestation of the real; we need only to realize that the real is not parcelled off and bounded as our language would make it seem. Certainly language is a reflection of the social reality that surrounds us. But to say that this social reality is a reality is not to say that it is the *only* manifestation of reality. There are different societies around the world. These societies are in constant change, flux, and conflicts. If everyone agreed that the world were formed in such-and-such a way, we would be at a loss to explain these conflicts. War results when the world-views of two groups are incapable of settling their ideological differences. If these ideologies were strictly translatable, then everyone would be in agreement as to how the world is really structured and there would be no conflict. Think of the crusades and other religious wars. The truth of each social reality is valid within its particular context, but when two social realities have literally to inhabit the same sphere (the earth) each party assumes that its ideology is the true ideology reflecting the nature of the real and those of others false. Instead of the conflict serving as an example of relative truth, and thereby allowing us safe passage, the conflict now serves only non-productive, destructive ends. When we use 'reality' in this context (social reality) we must remember that this reality is yet another manifestation of the real. Each social reality has its own language formed in its own particular circumstances. Language and thought (or language-thought) arise concurrently with the constantly evolving social phenomena. This is why any change in a subgroup of a culture is reflected by a change in the sub-language of that culture ("are you hip ?" "dig it ?") Were we to voice this question 50 years ago we would have gotten the answer, "No, me whole person."

Is the world then merely a disconnected scramble when we view it in terms of relative truth ? No, relative truth allows us clarity and pragmatic efficacy as to the nature of things such as conflicts, language and thought.

If we learn *all* the languages of the world, will we then know what reality is ? Not at all. The collection of relative truths, no matter how many, cannot have any ultimate status. We have seen that according to the Madhyamaka all these truths are relative truths. The higher truth is that even this insight is relative, in the sense that it is not descriptive of the real, but descriptive only of the matrix in which language and thought arise. Even the higher truth and the lower truth of the Madhyamaka are mutually dependent. Some philosophers might criticise the lower truth by saying that if this truth itself is relative, then we must not take it seriously, for it is not a *true* statement about the world. But when we consider the lower truth along with the higher truth, the resultant view is not a statement of the real, but a statement of the very nature of language and thought in general. It is important to note here that a truth is relative does not mean that it is useless. Quite the contrary, relative truth enables us a fluidity of thought, and the freedom to experience those places (if any description is to be given them) where language does not penetrate. Of course, our a priori preclusion of such possibilities inhibits and tends to cancel any reason to consider truths as anything other than absolute. The possibility of a mode of consciousness in a realm outside that of language and thought is the light in which we understand relative truth. But to ask "Is this realm real ?" is to be missing the boat, since like "truth," "real" is an aspect of the language-thought polarity and not an aspect of the world. Even using the phraseology "aspect of the world" is misleading since aspect itself presupposes a multiplicity. Presupposing a multiplicity would cast this thesis to the dialectical lions of the prasaṅga (Nāgārjuna's dialectic), if this multiplicity were taken as ultimate. This is only a way of speaking about things.

In order to explicate this dependence of thought and language and to show that there is much more to the existence of man than is circumscribed by thought and language, Don Juan introduces an eight-point diagram.

> The diagram in the ashes had two epicenters; one he called 'reason,' the other, 'will.' 'Reason' was interconnected directly with a point he called 'talking.' Through 'talking,' 'reason' was indirectly connected to three other points, 'feeling,' 'dreaming' and 'seeing.' The other epicenter, 'will,' was directly connected to 'feeling,' 'dreaming,' and 'seeing'; but only indirectly to 'reason' and 'talking'. . .
>
> 'These points represent a human being and can be drawn in any way you want.'
>
> 'Do they represent the body of a human being ?' I asked.
>
> 'Don't call it a body,' he said. 'These are eight points on the fibers of a luminous being. A sorcerer says, as you can see in the diagram, that a human being is, first of all, 'will,' because will is directly connected to three points, 'feeling,' 'dreaming' and 'seeing'; then next, a human being is 'reason.' This is properly a center that is smaller than will; it is connected only with talking.[1]

Even considering only six points of his eight-pointed diagram, it is clear that while Don Juan refers to thought and language as being "directly connected," and efficacious in the makeup of a human being, nonetheless, this is not all there is to human existence.

> 'We may say that every one of us brings to the world, eight points. Two of them, 'reason' and 'talking,' are known by everyone. 'Feeling' is always vague, but somehow familiar. But only in the world of sorcerers does one get fully acquainted with 'dreaming,' 'seeing' and 'will.' And finally, at the outer edge of that world, one encounters

1. Carlos Castaneda, *Tales of Power* (New York: Simon and Schuster, 1974), pp. 98-99.

the other two. The eight points make the totality of oneself.'[1]

When Castaneda asks further of the remaining two points, Don Juan replies,

> 'Those two points will never yield to 'talking' or to 'reason,' he said. Only 'will' can handle them. 'Reason' is so removed from them that it is utterly useless to try figuring them out. This is one of the hardest things to realize; after all, the forte of 'reason' is to reason out everything.'[2]

We do not wish at this point to get into a detailed discussion of the eight points that comprise the totality of a being. This will be discussed in a later chapter. All we wish to show now is that we only need to de-absolutize our categories, to make them relative, and our view of the world is larger than that composed by thought and language. If we a priori rule out the mystic, as Schaff has done, then our categories remain solid and absolute and our world is captured therein. Only when we have an inkling of something more than this can we deem these categories as relative:

> We are perceivers. We are an awareness; we are not objects; we have no solidity. We are boundless. The world of objects and solidity is a way of making our passage on earth convenient. It is only a description that was created to help us. We, or rather our 'reason,' forget that the description is only a description and thus we entrap the totality of ourselves in a vicious circle from which we rarely emerge in our lifetime.[3]

Language and thought then are two aspects of the human being. These two aspects are "directly connected," i.e. mutually dependent, and give us our everyday picture of the world. Thought and language create and maintain the everyday

1. Carlos Castaneda, *Tales of Power* (New York: Simon and Schuster, 1974), p. 99.
2. ibid., p. 99.
3. ibid. p., 100.

world. When we cease to maintain this thought and language, this world collapses and we are able to feel or, more generally, experience other planes that are ruled over by the other six points of a human being, just as language and thought rule over this one. As we shall see in a later chapter, a "man of knowledge" slips between these planes effortlessly. "Effortlessly" here means the equality of efficaciousness of the planes. That is, while some of these planes are certainly more primordial in nature (e.g. 'power'), all experiences are equal in that they appear in *some form or other*.

CHAPTER V

THE METAPHYSICS OF DON JUAN: HIS CONCEPTION OF REALITY

> I gave you enough of the sorcerer's view without letting you get hooked on it. I said that only if one pits two views against each other can one weasel between them to arrive at the real world. I meant that one can arrive at the totality of oneself only when one fully understands that the world is merely a view, regardless of whether that view belongs to an ordinary man or to a sorcerer.[1]

Carlos Castaneda's apprenticeship led him through the lands of the tonal and nagual, lands inhabited by sorcerers, men of knowledge, warriors, allies and phantoms; power places, power objects and personal power; luminous spheres, lines of the world, and the will. He made connections with these lands through "strange" practices such as, "the gait of power," "walking" and "dreaming," etc. While all of these activities, places and things are strange and illusory to us, the readers, unless we are familiar with lung-gompa and the Tri-kāya practices of Tibet, through the skilful pen of Castaneda they take on a concreteness of their own. These experiences and practices have taken on meanings in their respective categoric frameworks.

Don Juan artfully made these experiences "real," thus leading Castaneda from one conceptual framework to another and back, only to say that the Man of knowledge really arrives noplace[2] except at "the totality of oneself."[3] It is time now to

1. Carlos Castaneda, *Tales of Power* (New York: Simon and Schuster, 1974), p. 240.
2. Carlos Castaneda, *Journey to Ixtlan* (New York: Simon and Schuster, 1972), p. 264.
3. Carlos Castaneda, *Tales of Power* (New York: Simon and Schuster, 1974), p. 13.

ask the inevitable, nagging question, "What is Don Juan's conception of the real?" Does he have any metaphysics? If so, is it one or many? These are extremely difficult questions and are never squarely addressed in Castaneda's writings. However, by piecing together various teachings from both Don Juan and the Mādhyamika, we will arrive at a conclusion, although, as might be suspected from earlier chapters, this conclusion will be pleasing neither to the absolutist nor to the relativist. The reason for this is simply that both absolutism and relativism are *views* of the world. The shrewd dialectician at this point would interject by saying that the concept, "view of the world," implies that there is a real world which can be viewed (experienced). Is this not, he continues, itself an absolutistic view? To this we shall reply, yes, this manner of looking at things is indeed an absolutistic view. This does not, however, mean that the nature of the real is absolute; on the contrary, it only means that no description (view) of the world can be absolute. The statement, " what-the-absolutist-and-relativist-claim-of-the-world-are-only-views-of-the-world," is not in itself a description of the world, rather, it is a statement about the natures of language and thought themselves. It is clear that this statement is not a statement descriptive of reality; per contra, it concerns only conceptualization couched in its necessary vehicle, namely, language. We say 'necessary,' because we cannot speak of the everyday world of process and attribute without referring to substance. Moreover, we cannot speak of relativity without likewise sneaking absolutism through the back door. But, as polite scholars, we plan to announce to the host(ess) that while we are entering the front door as relativists, our constant companion, absolutism, is arriving via the humbler route. This is another way of saying that any discourse about absolutism and relativism may take a relativistic or absolutistic posture, as long as it is remembered that absolutism and relativism are relative to one another, and when taken as absolute in themselves become self-stultifying. That is, no view can be posited on our island of language without necessarily referring to the opposing view. This is not some dubious adaptation of an equal media time for candidates ruling, but a natural outcome of the Mādhyamika dialectic concerning thought in general. All views of the world are false if taken as absolute and exclusive; this simply means that the claim to absolute truth of any conceptual framework, in general, can be shown to be self-contradictory. This is necessarily so, because any concept C can only be explicated in terms of non-C. For example, if everything in the world were yellow, 'yellow' would be meaningless, since there would be nothing that is non-yellow with which to contrast. And in this respect, the contrasting item must (in the logical sense) be every bit as "real" (or "unreal") as the object itself. Likewise when we refer to conceptual frameworks, each framework is as true or false as its conceptual antithesis. Each thesis is logically necessary for the statement of the other. We can say that these theses are true only relatively but false and self-contradictory if claimed to be absolute. It also means that since any collection must, for the purposes of articulation, be in contrast with some *other* conceptual schemata, no collection of views, no matter how elaborate, can be considered an exhaustive description of the world.

If we incorporate the second schemata within the first (since we realize that the second is as necessary as the first), we generate a third conceptual schema in contrast to the first two; and so on ad infinitum. In our attempt to "nail down the world" by incorporating all possible concepts, we find ourselves falling victim to an infinite progression. If we are to look at views as relative and therefore equal, then language "explodes" in the attempt to articulate the real, just as mathematics did in chapter 3. This is in fact the implication of the Mādhyamika dialectic. All views are equal in that they are relative statements. They are empty (śūnyatā) in this respect, but nonetheless "true" descriptions of the world, and therefore not useless. I say "true" descriptions of the world in the strictly pragmatic sense that it serves certain purposes for us to conceptualize our experiences in certain ways. Others might find it useful to conceptualize experience differently. This, too, would yield a "true" but different description.

Therefore, when we say that "views of the world are relative" is an absolutistic statement, we mean absolutism is necessary for the articulation of relativity. This says nothing of the real, but only something of conceptual thinking.

All views are equally "true" in this sense of mutual dependence, but equally "false" in the sense that all views, if claimed to be absolute, are self-contradictory. The constituents of a description are not then "real" constituents of the world (for we cannot even assume a multiplicity of constituents) but rather they are really constituents of our language.

. . . .

We shall now address ourselves to the question whether or not Don Juan himself has a metaphysics (conception of reality), and if so, what is its nature. This will be a difficult subject to investigate since the bulk of the writing in Castaneda's four books discusses the experiences of Castaneda. Don Juan heralded the events in such a fashion that the experiences themselves were very "real" i.e., as real as any other experiences. In addition, Castaneda's writing expertise makes them all the more vivid. For these reasons, one can come to the easy conclusion that Don Juan has a fixed notion of what reality is really like. We have quoted him as saying that language is only a description. Of what is it a description ? Is the sorcerer's world where one "sees," the real world ? Or, is this not the message which Don Juan is conveying ?

When philosophers speak of metaphysics, usually they speak in terms of absolutes. These are the absolutes which are necessary to make any thesis "click." We must have a basic set of truths on which to build. Whenever a daring soul might bring the notion of relative truth into conversation, he (she) might be briefly honored for bravery, yet quickly and summarily dismissed on grounds ranging from question-begging to skepticism. Just as for Einstein, Nature does not "shoot craps," so, too, for the bulk of philosophy, the real world cannot be composed of relatives. Why, therefore, bother with talk of relativity with any respect to the real ? How can it tell us anything ? If relativity of truths has no bearing on the real, how can it have any philosophical bearing at all ? This is all too easy a conclusion to come to, especially if one is already committed to some faith or other. A cursory reader might object saying that Don Juan himself is a member of the faithful i.e., those faithful to the world of sorcery. We shall show that such an objection rests on a mistaken interpretation of Don Juan.

First of all Don Juan uses the concept of relativity of thought in order for Castaneda to realize that the world is not as our language portrays. Secondly, he teaches Castaneda techniques which make possible the actual penetration of the world behind language and thought and into the sorcerer's world, the sorcerer's world itself being governed by its own rules and descriptions. Are we to conclude then that the sorcerer's world, the nagual, is *the* real ? Not at all.

> . . . Today I have to pound the nail that Genaro put in, the fact that we are luminous beings. We are perceivers. We are an awareness; we are not objects; we have no solidity. We are boundless. *The world of objects and solidity is a way of making our passage on earth convenient. It is only a description that was created to help us.* We, or rather our "reason," forget that the description is only a description and thus we entrap the totality of ourselves in a vicious circle from which we rarely emerge in our lifetime.
>
> . . . We are perceivers, he proceeded. The world that we perceive, though, is an illusion. It was created by a description that was told to us since the moment we were born. We, the luminous beings, are born with two rings of power, but we use only one to create the world. That ring, which is hooked very soon after we are born, is "reason," and its companion is "talking." *Between the two they concoct and maintain the world.*
>
> So, in essence, the world that your reason wants to sustain is *the world created by a description and its dogmatic and inviolable rules, which the "reason" learns to accept and defend.*
>
> The secret of luminous beings is that they have another ring of power which is never used, the "will." The trick of the sorcerer is the same trick of the average man. *Both have a description*; one, the average man, upholds it with his reason; the other, the sorcerer, upholds it with his "will." *Both descriptions have their rules and the rules are perceivable, but the advantage of the sorcerer is that "will" is more engulfing than reason.*[1]

---

1. Carlos Castaneda, *Tales of Power* (New York: Simon and Schuster, 1974), pp. 100-101, emphasis added.

It is clear then that according to Don Juan one could not get at the real by sorcery. Were one to think that the rules of sorcery are descriptive of the real in an absolute sense and live by them alone, one would get too deeply immersed in a new view.[1] The world of sorcery then is bound up with yet another view.

To speak in terms of philosophy, Don Juan has developed what we can call a "metaphysics of relativity." To deal with the world, we must have some metaphysics or other. However, this metaphysics need not be one, nor ultimate (ultimately true) in any sense.

> Whenever you are in the world of the "tonal," you should be an impeccable tonal; *no time for irrational crap*. But whenever you are in the world of the nagual, you should also be impeccable; *no time far rational crap*. For the warrior, intent is the gate in between. It closes completely behind him when he goes either way.[2]

Don Juan's metaphysics then contains rationality as part and parcel of it with respect to certain frameworks (ordinary reality), and relegates it to "crap" in another. Conceptual knowledge, which is as true as can be in our everyday life, is a non-factor in the sorcerer's world. But likewise, the relations which hold "true" in the non-ordinary realm of the sorcerer need not necessarily hold in our everyday life. Each has an element of truth (i.e. their truths are relative with respect to their respective frameworks), but no ultimate truth in the sense of absolute and exclusive. The real can be captured neither with the conceptual apparatus of the ordinary man, nor with that of the sorcerer. The truths of the ordinary man and those of the sorcerer are only relative truths, (śūnyatā; empty of any absolute and ultimate content).

What, then, is the "real"? The "real" is a linguistic entity. It is the necessary and opposite pole which we need in order to speak of the notions of thought and language. The "real" is an item of the tonal (realm of nāma and rūpa, names and

1. Carlos Castaneda, *Tales of Power* (New York: Simon and Schuster, 1974), p. 239.
2. ibid., p. 173, emphasis added.

forms). However, we are dissatisfied with this answer alone since all traces lead toward some experience outside of language and thought. The experiences of the sorcerer, the experience of the "nagual" is also "real," relative to its own conceptual framework, and not that of the tonal.

What gives the right then to use the same term "real," with respect to both the "tonal," and the "nagual"? According to Don Juan, tonal and nagual are both legitimate and relative conceptual frameworks. When we say that the experiences of the "nagual" are real, we mean that the "nagual" is a conceptual framework in which one can operate (be efficacious). It would be a mistake to interpret this as saying that "real" is a term which has meaning with respect to the "nagual" itself. After all, the "nagual" cannot be described in terms of the "tonal," and "real" is a term of the tonal.

Are we then at an impasse in our attempt to discover in Don Juan's world what it is, if anything, that lies for us outside of form ? Note that anything that could be said about this realm could only be metaphoric and have no ultimate impact; but, after all, Don Juan does reach farther than the realm of metaphysics, as will be seen presently.

. . . . . .

Throughout Castaneda's attempts to deal with the "nagual," Don Juan constantly advised him not to "look into" the "nagual" (i.e. to impose names and forms—nāma and rūpa). Why is this so ?

> The ally is something which is outside of that view, outside the realm of 'reason.' It can be witnessed only at the center of 'will' at times when our ordinary view has stopped, therefore it is properly 'nagual.' *Sorcerer's, however, can learn to perceive the ally in a most intricate way, and in doing so they get too deeply immersed in a new view.* So, in order to protect you from that fate, I did not emphasize the ally as sorcerers usually do. Sorcerers have learned after generations of using power plants to account in their views for everything that is accountable about them. I would say that sorcerers, by using their 'will,' have succeeded in enlarging their views of the world. My teacher and benefactors were the clearest examples of that. *They were men af great power, but*

> *they were not men of knowledge. They never broke the bounds of their enormous views and thus never arrived at the totality of themselves. yet they knew about it.*[1]

Don Juan wanted Castaneda to experience the nagual, but not to dwell on it because he would just be "hooking" himself to a new view, larger but nonetheless a view, handled most generically in the sorcerer's explanation.[2] The sorcerer's explanation is as follows: We are born inside a bubble which is open, but closes as we begin to conceptualize. The bubble is our perception and conception in which we live, and it is no wonder that we see only our reflection on the inside of the bubble.

> The thing reflected is *our* view of the world, he said.
> That view is first a description, which is given to us from the moment of our birth until all our attention is caught by it and the description becomes a view.[3]

The bubble is then opened by the being's benefactor in order for him to "view his totality." "Naturally this business of calling it a bubble is only a way of talking, but in this case it is an accurate way."[4] The teacher then orders the elements of the "tonal" on one half of the bubble which is the side of "reason."

> . . . and by presenting him on the other hand with *unthinkable but real* situations, which the apprentice cannot cope with, he forces him to realize that his 'reason,' *although it is a most wonderful affair*, can only cover a small area.
> . . . The other half of the bubble, the one that has been cleared, can then be claimed by something sorcerers call 'will.'[5]
> Half of the bubble is the ultimate center of reason, the 'tonal.' The other half is the ultimate center of will,

1. Carlos Castaneda, *Tales of Power* (New York: Simon and Schuster, 1974), p. 239, emphasis added.
2. ibid. p. 247.
3. ibid. p. 247.
4. ibid. p. 247.
5. ibid. p. 248, emphasis added.

> the 'nagual.' That is the order that should prevail; any other arrangement is nonsensical and petty, because it goes against our nature; it robs us of our magical heritage.[1]

The sorcerer's explanation then is that we have two parts, "tonal" (reason) and "nagual" (will). For those who live in ordinary reality alone their being can be represented as totally "tonal" and inside a bubble which reflects the "tonal" to itself in perception. In this way it can be said that what we think is the world is actually a production of our own. But by living the life of a warrior (see chapter 6) one can order the items of the "tonal" on one half of the bubble, while the "will" rises in dependent origination (after all, this is only a view, and all views rise in dependent origination).

Don Juan's message is that one should view "tonal" and "nagual" as views of *something*, and to achieve a glimpse of that something, one has to "weasel between" these views. That something is what Don Juan refers to as the "totality of oneself."[2]

> Both of them repeated countless times in my ears that the nagual by itself was of no use, that it had to be tempered by the tonal.[3]

. . . . . .

Don Juan took Castaneda through the appropriate experiences bearing upon the sorcerer's explanation, including that of experiencing himself as a bundle of perceptions that could be expanded and brought together again. An adept sorcerer can arrange and rearrange these bundles. Thus, for instance, an adept can be aware of the "here" and the "there" at once. "The cluster of feelings can be made to assemble instantly anywhere."[4]

> Is this then Reality ? Still not ! Real is indescribable. Sorcerer's do the same thing with their 'will,' he said. They say that through the 'will' they can witness the effects of

---

1. Carlos Castaneda, *Tales of Power* (New York: Simon and Schuster, 1974), p. 248.
2. ibid., p. 254.
3. ibid., p. 253.
4. ibid., p. 268.

> the 'nagual.' I can add now that through 'reason,' no matter what we do with it, or how we do it, we are merely witnessing the effects of the 'tonal.' In both cases there is no hope, ever, to understand or to explain what it is that we are witnessing.[1]

Nāgārjuna also refers to this relativity of relativity (śūnyatā-śūnyatā) in the Mahā-Prajñāpāramitā-śāstra.[2] He teaches that it is the skilfulness of a Buddha to live between two worlds.

> *To live in the world and yet be free from defilements*, to retain individuality and yet be free from the false sense of self, to work for the world and yet be free from pride and passion—this is the skilfulness of the Buddha. . .[3]

Nāgārjuna refers to the higher and the lower as two aspects of a being:

> The sense of 'I' is not in itself false, although it belongs to the world of the determinate. As a mundane truth it refers to the complex of personality. Self reference as a reference to the real self, i.e., the real nature of one's being, is only one side of the sense of 'I.' For it is at the same time a reference to the divided, relative entity with which the being identifies itself as 'I,' and this entity, thus becomes the 'self' of the being; the life of the being consists in the life of this entity with which it has identified itself. From the standpoint of this specific entity, the body-mind complex, the being differentiates itself from all the rest as the not-self. This is the ordinary empirical self.[4]

Further, "*It shares at once two orders of being, the conditioned and the unconditioned.*"[5]

---

1. Carlos Castaneda, *Tales of Power* (New York: Simon and Schuster, 1974), p. 270.
2. K. Venkata Ramanan, *Nāgārjuna's Philosophy as Presented in the Mahā-Prajñāpāramitā-Śāstra* (Bharatiya Vidya Prakashan, 1971), p. 42.
3. ibid., p. 69, emphasis added.
4. ibid., p. 101.
5. ibid., p. 100.

In verse 370 a-b of the Śāstra, Nāgārjuna explains what is, in his terms (prajñāpāramitā), the Middle Way (Mādhyamika); and in terms of Don Juan, it is the sorcerer slipping between the two worlds.

> ... Ignorance is one extreme, extinction of ignorance is another; birth and death is one extreme, cessation of birth and death is another; that all things are existent is one extreme, that all things are non-existent is another. *Abandoning these two extremes to fare on the Middle Way, this is prajñāpāramitā.* Bodhisattva is one extreme, the six pāramitās are another; the Buddha is one extreme, the bodhi is another. Abandoning these two extremes to fare the Middle Way, this is *prajñāpāramitā.* To put the matter briefly, the six internal senses are one extreme, the six external objects are another; abandoning these two extremes to fare on the Middle Way, this is *prajñāpāramitā.* That this is *prajñāpāramitā* is one extreme, that this is not *prajñāpāramitā* is another extreme; *to abandon these two extremes and to fare the Middle Way, this is prajñāpāramitā.*[1]

So, too, for Nāgārjuna it is important for the bodhisattva not to cling to any extreme, but to slide between the extremes in order to achieve prajñāpāramitā (intuitional insight).[2] The bodhisattva should "go between" even the duality of "mundane" (saṃvṛti, tonal) and "ultimate" (paramārtha, nagual).

These same thoughts are expressed by Rechungma, a female disciple of Tibet's great yogi, Milarepa, in *The Hundred Thousand Songs of Milarepa.*

> The Three Precious Ones[3] are but one Entity;
> Amongst (the deities) I cannot discriminate.
> In the Pith-Instructions of whispered Lineage given by my Guru

1. K. Venkata Ramanan, *Nāgārjuna's Philosophy as Presented in The Maha-Prajnaparamita-Sastra* (Bharatiya Vidya Prakashan, 1971), p. 108.
2. ibid. p. 134.
3. The three bodies of Buddha, the Tri-Kāya: Dharmakāya: the body of forms; the Sambhogakāya: body of the Bodhisattva; and the Nirmāṇakāya: the formless Divine body of Truth.

There are no playwords or vain babblings.
In the practice of the Yidham Yoga,
Whose essence is the Jetsun,
There are no periods of time or intervals.
Things as they manifest are by nature magic-like;
I do not deem them to be substantial,
Nor do I cling to them with habitual thoughts !
In the mind-Essence, the quinte-sential 'light,'
There is no adulteration by distracting thoughts.
In the real nature of beings, the realm of Mind,
There is no subject-object defilement.
In the natural state of the Mind-Essence
There is no ground from which habitual thought may rise.[1]

Milarepa later himself puts it as follows:

. . . As form and Void into one are merged,
My mind is at ease and full of joy.
I am very happy
For I never fall into the trap
Of mere conceptualization of the Void. . .[2]

It is clear that the real for Don Juan, Nāgārjuna and Milarepa is a linguistic entity used to refer to a state wholly outside words and forms: a state which can only be experienced and never talked about, since talking entails conceptualization and thereby duality. Words are only pointers, and as such should never be clung to.

It can then be said that Don Juan, Nāgārjuna, as well as Milarepa, have *no* Metaphysics when taken in the classical sense of "ultimate truths" but a relativistic sense of Metaphysics, in that certain conceptual frameworks are more appropriate for dealing with one's surroundings. For the Yaqui Indian and Castaneda it is the framework of the "warrior," for Milarepa it is the framework of the "lonely traveller."

1. Garma C. C. Chang, trans. : *The Hundred Thousand Songs of Milarepa* (New York, Harper and Row, 1962), pp. 139-140.
2. ibid., p. 157, emphasis added.

If there can be said to be one universal guiding principle it is that of "being impeccable". This will be discussed in Chapter 6.

To complete the comparison, we would like to enter one last quote from Don Juan which incorporates the void which is mentioned above by Milarepa. This is possibly the most sweeping statement that Don Juan can make.

> Last night Genaro and I showed you the last two points that make the totality of men, the 'nagual' and the 'tonal'. I once told you that those two points were outside of oneself and yet they were not. That is the paradox of the luminous beings. The 'tonal' of every one of us is but a reflection of that indescribable unknown filled with order; *the 'nagual' of every one of us is but a reflection of that indescribable void that contains everything.*[1]

1. Carlos Castaneda, *Tales of Power* (New York: Simon and Schuster, 1974), pp. 270-271, emphasis added.

Chapter VI

DON JUAN'S CONCEPTION OF MAN AS "WARRIOR"

This is your world. You can't renounce it. It is useless to get angry and feel disappointed with oneself. All that that proves is that one's *tonal* is involved in an internal battle; a battle within one's *tonal* is one of the most inane contests I can think of. The tight life of a warrior is designed to end that struggle. From the beginning I have taught you to avoid wear and tear. Now there is no longer a war within you, not as it used to be, because the warrior's way is harmony—the harmony between actions and decisions, at first, and then the harmony between *tonal* and *nagual*.[1]

Life has to change into a thing vast and calm and intense and powerful that can no longer recognize its old blind eager narrow self or petty impulse and desire. Even the body has to submit to a mutation and be no longer the clamorous animal or the impeding clod it now is, but become instead a conscious servant and radiant instrument and living form of the spirit.[2]

Only from this intimate relationship of body and mind is it possible to understand the *siddhis* of bodily perfection, which have been reported again and again in the biographies of Buddhist saints—very much in contrast with the generally accepted idea of a body-reviling, ascetically-

1. Carios Castaneda, *Tales of Power* (New York: Simon and Schuster, 1974), p. 156.
2. Lama Anagarika Govinda, *Foundations of Tibetan Mysticism* (New York: Samuel Weiser, Inc., 1969), p. 70.

intellectual Buddhism which has crept into the historical and philosophical representations of the *Buddha-Dharma*.[1]

Thus far we have spoken of Don Juan and Nāgārjuna strictly intellectually. That is, we have discussed their logic, metaphysics and non-ordinary reality in much the same way as most philosophers would approach these matters. One might wonder whether the teachings of these men have any bearing on our everyday lives. As good Mādhyamika students, we consider this only a view, but like all views, there is a grain (and in this case a rock) of truth to it. I do not think it too sweeping a statement to make that Western philosophers, notwithstanding Kant, Leibnitz, or Russell, have not shown the connection between what they have to say and the mundane world of sweat and toil and laughter and fun.

It seems that philosophy has spent its time trying to say something about the "real" which is, as we have shown, indescribable. True, phenomena are only appearances, but they are the only appearances we have. Let us take issue here then and say that the phenomenal is as real or unreal as *the language* one may be speaking *would permit*. In addition, any concept describing such phenomena would be as true or false as its opposite (dependent origination).

What this means is that neither the mundane nor the non-mundane is subordinate to the other. After all, the trick of the "Man of Knowledge" is to "slip between" the two, going back and forth between the tonal and the nagual with great ease. Although Western scholarship has built brilliant and eloquent architechtonic, its vision of man and world is narrow, confining, dogmatic, and riddled with paradoxes and absurdities. The greatest of the paradoxes is that philosophers have systematically ignored any connections between ourselves as phenomenal beings and any realm of the "No-I". For those who argue that philosophy is strictly intellectual, we can only say that we do not care to make such delimitations on our study. The mind and the body are only views, and so is the "Non-mind". So to delineate a study to one or the other is necessarily non-unifying and pernicious. "Non-unifying" here means that any study which

1. Lama Anagarika Govinda, *Foundations of Tibetan Mysticism* (New York: Samuel Weiser, Inc., 1969), p. 70.

strictly delineates its scope purposefully (or otherwise) to the mundane, or the non-mundane, or any extreme, logically rules itself out of any unity with the other realm. Philosophers seem not to realize that nature does not speak philosophy and communicate on that level. It is certainly pernicious in that it breeds ill-being, fragmentation, and alienation.

But we cannot really blame philosophy for this, for what else is there to do, but talk ? People seek unifying principles, but they seek these principles in talk.

Don Juan abhors talk, but later admits that talk is the only tool that we as "tonals" (phenomenal beings) have to get at the real.[1] He earlier feigns talk to show Castaneda that sticking strictly to the world of talk forces us to think that talk is all there is. When he later says that it (talk) is the only tool that we have, he means that if we perform this talk impeccably, i.e. unclingingly, then it can lead us to the real.

Don Juan not only speaks of the tonal as equal to the nagual, but also gives a unifying principle which enables one to clean his tonal, i.e. live properly, and later act in the world of the sorcerer (nagual) and still later unify both "tonal" and "nagual". This unifying principle to which we refer is that of living like a "warrior".

It is truly unfortunate that we have many years of the media which have engrained various prejudiced connotations of the word "warrior" in reference to the American Indian. The word itself is tinged with the conception of a fighter or killer. In the many movies that we have seen, the "brave" aspires to the long arduous task of becoming a warrior. For all of Hollywood's perversion and distortion of what apparently was a strong belief among Indians, two things do come through; one, the process was long and arduous, involving some sort of stoic attitude, and two, perfection was the aim and end.

We are not hereby declaring that the cowboy movies of yesteryear are in any way an accurate account of what transpired among tribes of American Indians. Quite the contrary. However, there are two aspects that seem to be hard to pervert when thought of in a general way, stoicism and perfection. Perfection in

1. Carlos Castaneda, *Tales of Power* (New York: Simon and Schuster, 1974), p. 265.

general means doing whatever the task may be in the best possible (non-clinging) manner, with the highest excellence, as Aristotle would say. Stoicism in general means meeting with whatever circumstances might present themselves with certainty and dispassion (in the best sense of the term).

Extrapolating in such a manner from the literature on the subject of American Indians, we can get the feeling of the impact the notion of "warrior" had on the American Indian.

This is far too general a task for an adequate representation in a short chapter, but we wish to further examine Don Juan's notion of "warrior". We also wish to compare this to the notion of mindfulness and one-pointedness in the life of the Bodhisattva in Buddhism since it is an exact parallel.

In Don Juan's system of knowledge, after the preliminaries are over with, and the teacher is sure the pupil is ready, the teacher embarks the student on the life of a hunter.[1]

While hunting, one learns the patterns of the hunted, which are employed in trapping the hunted. The hunter is humble enough to realize that the hunted is on a par with him and capable of turning the tables on the hunter. So as not to become the hunted, the hunter must erase *all* habits. For example, one must sleep and thereby become vulnerable. The hunter therefore continuously changes his time and places of rest. The impeccability of the hunter of course necessitates that the whole enterprise be non-wasteful.

While hunting, the hunter learns the technique of "letting go, but not letting go."[2] This is the development of the non-attachment necessary in the concentration of total energy for the task, and yet a "holding on" in having complete control over the situation.

In Castaneda's experience, the technique was precipitated by an excruciatingly frightful experience; but Don Juan noted that once it happened, the hunter could notice how it happens and perform it whenever necessary. These exoteric aspects

1. Carlos Castaneda, *Journey to Ixtlan* (New York: Simon and Schuster, 1972), p. 74 ff.

2. Ibid., p. 119.

of hunting are reterred to by Don Juan as the "outside forms of hunting."[1]

Don Juan deftly turns Castaneda's experience of hunting for game into its esoteric counterpart of hunting for "power". "As I told you, a warrior is an impeccable hunter that hunts power."[2] "Power" will be discussed in a later chapter, but suffice it for now to say that in this sense Don Juan means not only "personal power", but a more generic "Power" which is the perpetual and mysterious flow of force underlying appearance. That is Don Juan's method of getting the apprentice to "peep behind" appearance, while not concentrating on making it into yet another appearance.

* * *

It is easy to see that the prop of the "hunter" is extremely handy to a teacher in Don Juan's milieu. After all, hunting and gathering as well as some farming is how American Indians sustained themselves so beautifully and self-reliantly for centuries. In another milieu, another exoteric "vikalpa" (skt. construction) could be used to carry the same message, but we hope to show later some surprising comparisons in non-Western thought with respect to this matter. Suffice it to say that for now total mindfulness and perfection of action are the keynotes in the life of a warrior, which can be performed in any but the most perverted social milieu.

When a hunter has learned to face "power" with abandon and yet control, he is ready to be a "warrior".

* * *

There is no sharp demarcation between "hunter" and "warrior". The path is continuous. However, we can say that once one reaches the "warrior" stage, he is capable of facing *any* task on his own without any attachment at all, either to views, fear, enlightenment or bravado. "A warrior is impeccable when he trusts his personal power regardless of whether it is small or enormous."[3]

---

1. Carlos Castaneda, *Journey to Ixtlan* (New York: Simon and Schuster, 1972), p. 74.
2. ibid. p. 107.
3. ibid. p. 168.

So a warrior may be young and relatively inexperienced and have accumulated only small merit, or older and relatively experienced and have accumulated much merit; but in either case, impeccability lies in trusting in whatever positive karma he or she has been able to affect to date. The result is that the warrior loses any feeling of helplessness in his dealings in the world. The warrior has the freedom to act, and after the act all results will naturally follow regardless of any attitudes of the actor. Therefore, all mental conduct with respect to the action is really extraneous and eventually debilitating.

The warrior must then take responsibility for the act (i.e. complete mindfulness of any act) and then live with the consequences whatever they might be. Consequences themselves are neither good nor bad, they merely follow. "Good" and "bad" are only judgments on our part made in order to convince ourselves that what we have done is acceptable to all (who are "important"). But these judgments are merely mindless meanderings when we view life from the eyes of a warrior. The act is done, the consequences will arise sooner or later; rejoicing or lamenting our decision is only to waste the time one has in the pursuit of perfection. The warrior knows that there will be a multitude of effects which arise in dependent origination with his action. These multitudes of effects are *not* like confetti which scatters in all directions with no pattern or binding force, but take their place in the infinite karmic river in which the warrior, and all of us for that matter, are immersed.

If the warrior acts impeccably, there is no aspect of this "karmic river" to which he is attached and the warrior is free to use the power of any facet of karma to its best possible advantage.

To use the appropriate Buddhist phraseology, then, we might explain it in the following fashion. Let us say that there are two individuals, A and B. Let us suppose that at a certain time both A and B were attached to a certain action or non-action, but for different reasons. Let us say that they are involved in an action, and this action arises from attachment to material goods. Both A and B voice the claim that material goods are "for the birds." Can we say that since both these men exhibit the same behavior, they must have the same psychological orientation ? The answer is no, and this is why behavioral psychology, used in isolation, is a deadend.

A has tried and tried in the business world to attain material goods. He has tried with all the means he can think of, and yet failed. At age 40 he declares that, "people are rats and you really have no control over the situation anyhow", and abruptly gives up his efforts to declare that he is going to become a hermit, and live out his days alone. B on the other hand sees that the business world, like any other path, unless handled in an impeccable manner, leads only to unhappiness. He sees his fellow workers as wholly unaware of impeccability, stabbing each other's back, thinking that this is the right action that will fulfil the dreamt-of wishes. Their original unhappiness of wanting objects is multiplied continuously by the pangs of conscience for the backstabbing and more effectively by the so-called "bad Karma" they produce in the lives of others.

Noticing this, B thinks that while he may try to be impeccable, the inability of those around him to follow the impeccable path is not under his control. In this scene of unhappiness B realizes that this path to riches only breeds unhappiness despite the fact that one might be "successful". B decides to drop all efforts in this direction. To the behaviorist, the two cases would be identical, but to claim so seems to leave out so much.

The difference between A and B is one of intention. We can say that A has "*resigned*" himself to what he perceived as the cruel world. B on the other hand has *renounced* the world. A slumps down in a corner admitting his inability and impotence with respect to the world; whereas B has declared his independence of material goods. B is "unattached" while A is "attached" to his own unattachment. The actions of both are the same, but one man is free while the other is bound. Were B to revel in his accomplishments, he would be giving this accomplishment an ultimate status and thereby "clinging" at a different level. This type of clinging is even more dangerous than the first.

> Denying yourself is an indulgence and I don't recommend anything of the kind. That is the reason why I let you ask all the questions you want. If I told you to stop asking questions, you might warp your will trying to do that. The indulgence of denying is by far the worst : it forces us to believe we are doing great things, when in effect we are only fixed within ourselves.[1]

But how can one deny oneself all material and psychological attachments ? One needs some push, something in the light of which makes these attachments small and petty. In order to show necessity in this path of knowledge, Don Juan taught Carlos how to use "death as an advisor."

Death is an unpopular topic, and usually talked about by only the morbid, such as undertakers and manic depressives. But morbidity arises only when a person has the time to dwell on such topics, and the warrior has no time for this. His death is too impending to worry about such nonsense The morbid individual allows this idea of death to harp on and lull him into inaction. The warrior on the other hand, uses impending death to remind himself that he has little time to perfect himself. Time wasted on such unimportant topics as worry only hinders the individual by that much.

The warrior, now armed with his healthy awareness of death, uses even his death, a seemingly negative affair, in a positive way; namely, as the catalyst necessary to achieve action. The action achieved is not any action, but the action of a man who knows he is going to die. So the action is never half-hearted or incomplete, but done with full concentration.

From all the talk of reincarnation in non-Western cultures one might get the impression that there is never any hurry or rush; since if perfection were not reached in this life, it could be achieved in the next.

Don Juan never mentions reincarnation. Can we then justify a comparison with non-Western thought ? It seems so. In this

---

1. Carlos Castaneda, *A Separate Reality* (New York: Simon and Schuster, 1971), p. 146.

respect, the teachings of Don Juan parallel those of the non-Western "short path." This short path is the achievement of Buddhahood in one lifetime. A master of the "short path" is the Tibetan Yogi, Milarepa. The following is a partial quotation of a song which Milarepa sang to a hunter whom he happened upon.

> Life flees fast. Soon death
> Will knock upon your door.
> It is foolish, therefore one's devotion to postpone.
> What else can loving kinsmen do
> But throw one into Saṁsāra?
> To strive for happiness hereafter
> Is more important than seek it now.
> The time has come for you to rely on a Guru,
> The time has come to practice Dharma.[1]

So, too, for Milarepa, there is no time to waste in the following of one's devotion. This is indeed a mysterious position for both Don Juan and Milarepa to assume. After all, ultimately both (as we have seen) declare time to be unreal and illusory. However, it is not so mysterious when we think of how individuals degenerate into vegetables when they think of themselves as immortal. When we think we have an infinity of time we are lulled into total inaction thinking that some rational tidbit of information might come to us at some time in the future and assist us in action. However, this only breeds inaction. To the warrior who is going to die only action counts. His action is the right action since it is done impeccably and unclingingly in the overarching presence of death. In the light of one's death, one cannot put off right action until tomorrow for sensory pleasures today since tomorrow one may not be alive to "set things right." Therefore today, now, right at this moment there must be perfect, impeccable action, for tomorrow one may not be here. Our death gives us the only reason not only for action but for impeccable action.

---

1. Garma C. C. Chang. trans., *The Hundred Thousand Songs of Milarepa* (New York: Harper and Row, 1962), p. 151.

In this way, Don Juan, Nāgārjuna, and Milarepa take the most negative aspect of our conceptual network, namely death, and turn it into the most powerful tool of perfection, the groundwork, for impeccable action. This is not morbid or juvenile. Quite the contrary, awareness of our death is the only means of achieving perfection. Morbidity comes only when death is clung to. The warrior has no time for such clinging. He has only time in which to act in accordance with the advisor. Death is neither good nor bad, but merely a phenomenal factor in all of our beings. Death is an integral part of life, in the sense that they both are governed by dependent origination. Those who cling to life, one side of the dichotomy, fail to recognize such to be the case and live their lives in inaction, never seeking enlightenment since they think that there is plenty of time for that. On the other hand, the morbid cling to death (the other end of the dichotomy) and are a kind of living dead who think that "life is just to die."[1]

The farer of the Middle Path (Mādhyamika) and the warrior do not cling to either of these extremes of eternalism and nihilism. The bodhisattva lives life with death in mind and dies with life in mind, but clings to neither, realizing that phenomenologically and conceptually the two are mutually dependent. The warrior neither fears death nor embraces life. The warrior is here, now, alive. Tomorrow he might be there, then, dead. Clinging to either extreme only inhibits the individual from living well and dying well.

Lama Govinda points out this same thing in his explanation of his Guru's preliminary teachings :

> The Guru then went on to explain some of the preconditions and preliminary exercises of meditation for bringing about this positive and creative attitude : Unselfish love and compassion towards all living beings was, according to him, the first prerequisite of meditation, as it removed all self-created emotional and intellectual limitations; and in order to gain this attitude one should look upon all beings like upon one's own mother or one's own children, since

1. Lou Reed, "Sweet Jane" (BMI Recordings), 1974.

> there was not a single being in the universe that in the infinity of time had not been closely related to us in one way or another. In order to be conscious of the preciousness of time *one should realise that any moment might be the last of this life* and that the opportunity which it offers might not come again easily.[1]

As the warrior exoterically steers clear of all clingings, there is no place where he may hang his hat and call home. In this way rather than clinging to a few elements of analysis, the warrior frees himself from any clinging, enabling him to accommodate all views and thereby hang his hat anywhere. This seems to be the foundation on which one can understand Don Juan's cryptic utterance, "... Upon learning to 'see' a man becomes everything by becoming nothing."[2]

With nothing to cling to, there is no-thing with which the warrior could identify himself. This enables the warrior to accommodate all views including the views of birth and death. Therefore the warrior who "sees" is really nothing since there is no category to which he clings (identify with), but somehow becomes "everything" being able to accommodate all views. Clinging to any view, including "Nirvāṇa" or "nagual," only stultifies the warrior's efforts toward complete akasa (accommodation).

Now, how can we take this notion of "warrior" as impeccable and weave it across all levels of apprenticeship and knowledge? Early in Castaneda's apprenticeship, Don Juan told him not to be afraid, since fear was only one of our natural enemies. According to Don Juan, man has four natural enemies :

1. Fear
2. Clarity
3. Power
4. Old age

1. Lama Anagarika Govinda, *The Way of the White Clouds* (Berkeley: Shambala Publications, Inc., 1970), pp. 34-35, emphasis added.
2. Carlos Castaneda, *A Separate Reality* (New York: Simon and Schuster, 1971), p. 153.

In order to be a "man of Knowledge" one must overcome all four natural enemies.

With regard to the first enemy, we have seen how Don Juan employs the method of "using death as an advisor." In this way the warrior combats fear of death by using death itself as a positive tool. The warrior does everything as if there is no tomorrow, and thereby impeccably.

When the warrior vanquishes fear, he is able to look at the contradictions of the world (fourfold negation dialectic, see Chapter 2) with great clarity, unafraid. The warrior is unafraid to explore these contradictions, and thereby attains clarity. The warrior's clarity allows him to peep into the darkest recesses of conceptual thought, and see the entirety of conceptual thought at once, in a flash. Conceptual schemata rise and fall before the warrior. But one must not succumb to the second enemy, clarity.

Clarity of thought is only a small portion of our possible experience; so the warrior should not cling to this clarity. The warrior's only choice is to use clarity when it is advantageous, but use it impeccably, remembering that the categories are only a veil. When asked how to overcome clarity, Don Juan replies :

> He must do what he did with fear : he must defy his clarity and use it only to see, and wait patiently and measure carefully before taking new steps ; he must think, above all, that his clarity is almost a mistake. And a moment will come when he will understand that his clarity was only a point before his eyes. And thus he will have overcome his second enemy. . .[1]

So the overcoming of the second enemy is the realization that power is what lies for us outside of language. "A man who is defeated by power dies without really knowing how to handle it."[2]

We will discuss power in a following chapter, but for now,

1. Carlos Castaneda, *Teachings of Don Juan: A Yaqui Way of Knowledge* (Berkeley: University of California Press, 1968), p. 85.

2. Ibid., p. 86.

> 'How can he defeat his third enemy, Don Juan ?'
>
> 'He has to defy it, deliberately. He has to come to realize the power he has seemingly conquered is in reality never his. He must keep himself in line at all times, handling carefully and faithfully all that he has learned. If he can see that clarity and power, without his control over himself, are worse than mistakes, he will reach a point where everything is held in check. He will know then when and how to use his power. And thus he will have defeated his third enemy.'[1]

So by being a warrior and handling power unclingingly, the warrior can become a man of knowledge by fending off the "invincible" final enemy, old age.

> 'But if the man sloughs off his tiredness, and lives his fate through, he can then be called a man of knowledge, if only for the brief moment when he succeeds in fighting off his last, invincible enemy. That moment of clarity, power, and knowledge is enough.'[2]

In the light of his death, the warrior relishes the clarity, power, and knowledge to become a "man of knowledge." And what are the external indications when a person has accomplished this last manoeuvre ? For the answer, we must skip from this (above) conversation near the beginning of Castaneda's first book, to the very end of Castaneda's last book.

> 'The life of a warrior cannot possibly be cold and lonely and without feelings,' he said, 'because it is based on his affection, his devotion, his dedication to his beloved. And who, you may ask, is his beloved ? I will show you now.'
>
> Don Genaro stood up and walked slowly to a perfectly flat area right in front of us, ten or twelve feet away. He made a strange gesture there. He moved his hands as if he

1. Carlos Castaneda, *Teachings of Don Juan : A Yaqui Way of Knowledge* (Berkeley : University of California Press, 1968), p. 87.

2. Ibid., p. 87.

were sweeping dust from his chest and his stomach. Then an odd thing happened. A flash of an almost imperceptible light went through him; it came from the ground and seemed to kindle his entire body. He did a sort of backward pirouette, a backward dive more properly speaking, and landed on his chest and arms. His movement had been executed with such precision and skill that he seemed to be a weightless being, a wormlike creature that had turned on itself. When he was on the ground he performed a series of unearthly movements. He glided just a few inches above the ground, or rolled on it as if he were lying on ball bearings; or he swam on it describing circles and turning with the swiftness and agility of an eel swimming in the ocean.

The sight was sublime. Then the ball of fire came to rest and stayed motionless. A voice shook me and dispelled my attention. It was don Juan talking. I could not understand at first what he was saying. I looked again at the ball of fire; I could distinguish only don Genaro lying on the ground with his arms and legs spread out.

Don Juan's voice was very clear. It seemed to trigger something in me and I began to write.

'Genaro's love is the world,' he said. 'He was just now embracing this enormous earth but since he's so little all he can do is swim in it. But the earth knows that Genaro loves it and it bestows on him its care. That's why Genaro's life is filled to the brim and his state, wherever he'll be, will be plentiful. Genaro roams on the paths of his love and, wherever he is, he is complete.'

Don Juan squatted in front of us. He caressed the ground gently.

'This is the predilection of two warriors,' he said. 'This earth, this world. For a warrior there can be no greater love.'

Don Genaro stood up and squatted next to don Juan for a moment while both of them peered fixedly at us, then they sat in unison, cross-legged.

'Only if one loves this earth with unbending passion can one release one's sadness,' don Juan said. 'A warrior is always joyful because his love is unalterable and his beloved,

> the earth, embraces him and bestows upon him inconceivable gifts. The sadness belongs only to those who hate the very thing that gives shelter to their beings.'[1]

This love is referred to by Garma Chang as the "Compassion of Buddhahood."

> Compassion of Non-discrimination or Non-discernment (T.T. : dMigs. Pa. Mei. Pahi. sNyin. rJe), is a spontaneous, non-discriminating, and infinite love embodied in the Uncreated Voidness—the exclusive Compassion of Buddhahood. From the human point of view, compassion cannot arise without an object about which it is concerned. Compassion or love seems necessarily to be involved in a dualistic or subject-object mode. But according to Mahāyāna Buddhism, the highest compassion is one that transcends both subject and object, and is brought forth through the realization of Voidness. It is, in essence, identical with the intuitive Wisdom-of-Voidness. This is one of the most inscrutable mysteries of Buddhahood.[2]

To shed further light,

> In states of rapture, trance and highest intuition, as characterized by the stages of deep absorption in meditation (dhyāna), we experience the *Dharmakāya* as the luminous forms of purely spiritual perception—as pure, eternal principles of form, freed from all accidentals—or as the exalted visions of a higher reality. In them the *Sambhogakāya* 'the Body of Bliss' is realized. From it flow all immortal art, all deep wisdom, all profound truths (*dharma*, in the sense of formulated or proclaimed truth). Its enjoyment is of two kinds, like that of every great work of art: the rapture of the creative act and the enjoyment of those who contemplate the completed work by retrospectively experiencing and reliving the act of creation.

1. Carlos Castaneda, *Tales of Power* (New York: Simon and Schuster, 1974), p. 283-285.
2. Garma C.C. Chang, trans., *The Hundred Thousand Songs of Milarepa* (New York: Harper and Row, 1962), p. 153.

A rapture, comparable to the first of these two kinds, is experienced by all the Buddhas and Bodhisattvas in the course of their *sādhana* and in the practice of the highest virtues (*pāramitā*), as demonstrated by their lives—while a rapture, comparable to the second kind, is felt by all those who contemplate the significance of these lives and relive them in their mind and their deeds.[1]

1. Lama Anagarika Govinda, *Foundations of Tibetan Mysticism* (New York: Samuel Weiser, Inc., 1969), p. 214.

CHAPTER VII

KNOWLEDGE AND POWER : THE PSYCHOLOGICAL TEACHINGS OF DON JUAN

The purpose of this chapter is to link the abstract "power", to which we allude, to the consummation of the path of Don Juan. However, this shall not be done in a predictable way. The predictable way, the "obvious" way, is to say that power is the sought-for gem, and knowledge is the knowledge of attainment. To force this interpretation upon either Don Juan or Nāgārjuna would be an injustice, even worse, a misinterpretation.

How so ? After all, it is certain that power was achieved by both Don Juan and Castaneda, and if knowledge was of no use in the attainment, then what good is knowledge ? This seems a plausible objection on the surface: however, we wish to show that if power were the sought-after achievement, then whoever does the achieving has to face the inevitability of clinging to the idea of power or the practice of power. Why ? Because if power is the end result of practice, then power would be an extreme. Why ? Because power would be the ultimate achievement and therefore the prize, the most substantial, the real.

If we say that this is so, we can only say that it is in a very limited frame of reference. If in previous chapters we have emphasized that extremes should be avoided, then it should be emphasized even more so in the case of power. We wish to show that while power is the most primordial concept in the teachings of Don Juan, it is still a concept. Yet it is not our intention to leave it hang as a concept. If strict conceptual analysis is insisted upon, our discussion will yield nothing further than a mere inspection of our language. Power cannot be captured so easily.

The term "power" as referred to by Don Juan lies at such extreme fringes of language, that it is impossible to uncover a referent. To apply a referent would drag the whole enterprise back into the mundane, and with reference to power, this is the last thing that should be done. Not even the *last* thing, it should not be done at all.

How can we then talk about a concept which has no referent, and still tread the Mādhyamika path, clear of the extremes of metaphysics ? The answer is simple. Power has *absolutely* nothing to do with metaphysics. Quite the contrary, according to Don Juan, power should be approached from the non-conceptual, non-ontological (see hunting for power).[1] One might say that this only fogs the issue. But that is just our point, the issue *should* be fogged, "fogged" in the following sense.

We see the everyday world as cut and dry. We see the world as duality, but we see it as a certain type of duality. We see the world as full of dichotomies. Black or white, good or bad, ugly or beautiful. In the above series we use the disjunct "or" instead of the conjunct "and" because behaviorally, this is how man operates. He divides the world and hops onto the side of whatever he has determined to be "good" or "bad", or "black" or "white". We envision the world as dichotomy, an unfortunate result of the principle of the excluded middle. A *or* not A. One must be the case, both cannot be. We visualize the world as dichotomy. (We hasten to add that the real is not adequately described by A and $\sim$A either.)

However, we do not wish to decry duality. We only wish to shed light upon another, more basic view of duality, namely "polarity". If we see the world as polarity instead of dichotomy, then we shall not be so eager to pick sides, for the sides simply vanish. To pretend to eliminate one side of a dichotomy by joining the ranks of another is absurd. Generically, the dichotomies which we describe are polarities. And as we shall hope to describe, these polarities are none other than power.

For example, suffering (dukkha) and freedom are generally thought of as dichotomies. Many aspire to eliminate suffering.

1. Carlos Castaneda *Journey to Ixtlan* (New York : Simon and Schuster, 1972), p. 121 ff.

This is because they see suffering as distinct. To see this as polarity means that one and the other (i.e. suffering and its absence) are in the same boat. Their only difference is that they are rowing in opposite directions. The ends of a polarity, rather than being distinct, are actually one. At the same time, however, there is a tension between the poles, and we "create" the world from this tension. It is the inextricable connection, the pull between the poles which exemplifies power. To cut this connection between poles and dichotomize, voids this tension between the poles, thereby narrowing our world to such an extent as to leave us completely and literally powerless.

This tension is only a way of speaking. In reality there is no tension, only power. We may choose to glide on the wings of power, or we may clip the wings by dichotomizing. We are free to choose. Don Juan, as we quoted in the previous chapter, said that the only free act of a warrior is to act impeccably. He defines an act of impeccability as an action which is performed concurrently with the thought of the fact that the actor is a mortal creature. That is, the warrior should never act as though he were immortal.

What could Don Juan be thinking of? Simply this, that even the duality of life and death should not be thought of as dichotomous; rather, it should be thought of as polarity. Could a warrior then choose the dichotomy over the polarity? It does not seem so because dichotomizing is a path only for immortals. After all, only an immortal being can afford the time to waste in play acting needless battles between opposites and the conceptual futility of attempting to eliminate one end of a polarity. The warrior on the other hand has only the time to use the polar tension to his best advantage.

To drive our point home, however, we are going to have to use a very unorthodox method. The method is as follows. We live in an upside down world, and as such we must think of power exactly the opposite, as has been explicated above. That is, until now we have implied that first (logically first) there is a polarity and then there is tension as a result; which is a specific form of power.

Let us now say that the opposite is more closely true. That is, that first there is power, which we then interpret as tension, which logically necessitates polarity. Let us further say that this backward logic is not "really" true, but neither is the frontward way of looking at things. But let us investigate what comes of the tension created between these backward and frontward logics by seeing them as poles (polar views), which are views, but views, that can point the way if neither is clung to.

So, first we say that we view things as dichotomy, i.e. opposites being distinct, mutually exclusive categories. Secondly, if we view this duality as polarity, the poles become as one, mutually dependent (*pratītyasamutpāda*). Since we are now seeing the poles as one, and yet referring to them as plural (poles), the nagging question is, "what is the difference between them?" The answer is that there is reallv no difference, but only a tension between them since they are the instances of power manifested as duality. However, the power of duality is lost in dichotomy. Small wonder, then, that Don Juan and Nāgārjuna insist that the ego must be lost in order to obtain insight. Why? Simply because even with other clingings completely banished, the ego forms the last frontier of dichotomy. It is the ego that separates us from the animals, plants, and the world in general. The concept of the ego insists that its holder believes that he is substantially different from the world.

The ego *is* an instance of power or a manifestation of power, but only power draining and not power continually flowing and replenishing. So, no matter what energy we can lay claim to by accomplishment, the very fact of laying claim is a product of the ego, and an instantaneous energy or power drain.

Were a person to view the world as polarity and not dichotomy, the logical limit would then be loss of ego. This loss, as we shall later see, is not total abandonment, but only a non-clinging to the concept of "ego" as indicative of the true nature of the self.

* * * *

Let us then take these two views of power and pit them against each other. Pit against, not in any violent and non-productive way, nor in the way that Marx intended to arrive at a third, "better" view, but pit in the sense that seeing the opposing views side by side will show us that concepts are limited with regard to this (and all) subjects.

First, let us say that:

View A: Duality is logically prior. If we express this duality as polarity, we presuppose a relationship between the poles. After all, if any two things are to be compared, they must have an element of commonality. This relationship we have called "tension". A scientific metaphor for this tension would be "force at a distance" (north-south). Sociologically, we see a most literal tension, which we call racial tension (black and white). Psychologically, we refer to this tension as "internal struggle" (ego-superego); and so on. So "tension" has an empirical foundation as well as logical. This "tension" between poles is then more generically "power". "Power" not in the naive sense of "word power" as seen in the TV and magazine advertisements, but power in the sense that only the poles in combination (and strictly *not* in isolation) have impact upon our study of the world. It should be noted that this is only one view, and like any other view, subject to contradiction when extended to logical limits. The contradiction would evolve if the notion of "tension" as a relation between two poles were taken seriously. After all, if polarity necessitates tension as a relation, then there must be a relation between the third theoretical entity (tension) and the two relata (poles in this case), and so forth ad infinitum. "Tension" then must not be clung to.

The logical limit of the "backward view" would be:

View B: The real is non-Dual, and only "power" exists. Power is non-dual. Since it is non-dual, we cannot immediately grasp it with our perceptual-conceptual framework(s) which breathes duality. Since we cannot conceptualize non-duality, we interpret this "power" as "tension." Tension presupposes a duality since tension takes place only between pairs. Thus we arrive at polarity.

Statement A has a more realistic bent while statement B a more idealistic one. But were we to cling to the non-dual we would be hard pressed to defend non-duality as ultimate. Why? Because concepts rise in dependent origination. We have nothing that serves as its opposite.

Dialectically, were we to opt for a monism (non-duality), then "all" must be included. Recalling our Kantian discussion of space-time being infinite, how can we logically commit "all there is" to the category of categories with nothing excluded? On the other hand, were we to exclude anything in our monism, then how can this monism be a "real" monism?

So neither view can be ultimately true, and yet both Castaneda and Nāgārjuna insist that by not clinging to either, one can experience the real.

The following is an excerpt from *Separate Reality*. It follows Don Juan's discussion of an episode in Castaneda's life which made a heavy impression. Castaneda felt helpless in improving a small boy's situation in life. Don Juan explained that only the boy could bring about change just as Castaneda had in his life.

> 'But how can he?'
>
> 'By learning to reduce his wants to nothing. As long as he thinks that he was a victim, his life will be hell. And as long as you think the same your promise will be valid. What makes us unhappy is to want. Yet if we would learn to cut our wants to nothing, the smallest thing we'd get would be a true gift. Be in peace, you made a good gift to Joaquin. To be poor or wanting is only a thought; and so is to hate, or to be hungry or to be in pain.'
>
> 'I cannot truly believe that, don Juan. How could hunger and pain be only thoughts?'
>
> 'They are only thoughts for me now. That's all I know. I have accomplished that feat. The power to do that is all we have, mind you, to oppose the forces of our lives; without that power we are dregs, dust in the wind.'
>
> 'I have no doubt that you have done it, don Juan, but how can a simple man like myself or little Joaquin accomplish that?'
>
> 'It is up to us as single individuals to oppose the forces of our lives. I have said this to you countless times: Only a warrior can survive. A warrior knows that he is waiting and what he is waiting for: and while he waits he wants nothing and thus whatever little thing he gets is more than he can take. If he needs to eat he finds a way, because he

is not hungry; if something hurts his body he finds a way to stop it, because he is not in pain. To be hungry or to be in pain means that the man has abandoned himself and is no longer a warrior; and the forces of his hunger and pain will destroy him.[1]

So according to Don Juan, suffering (dukkha) comes from wanting. According to the *Śāstra*, "Although each view has its own distinctness, the false sense of self is the root (of all other false views.)[2] In addition, Ramanan, sighting the *Śāstra*, 294-6, 697a and others, observes

> *The tendency to seize is the root of conflict and suffering* : This situation seems to have provided for Nāgārjuna but one instance of the inveterate tendency of the human mind, the tendency to cling, to seize.[3]

So in order to minimize one's own suffering, we must, according to Don Juan and Nāgārjuna, sever the "wanting strings," which we construct between ourselves and views, objects and ultimately the false notion of the I. This is of course entailed in leading the life of a "warrior." By eliminating the clinging to objects we free ourselves to "see" what lies behind the object. By not clinging to views, we free ourselves to let views point toward "power." By not clinging to ego we free ourselves to unite with all else that exists and experience power. It should be noted that the above actions might not be sufficient conditions for one's realization of power, but they are certainly necessary.

If we would care to, we could extend the argumentation for the precedence of either view A or B as being self contradictory via Nāgārjuna's prasaṅga (four corner negation). It would outline as follows :

---

1. Carlos Castaneda, *A Separate Reality* (New York : Simon and Schuster, 1971), p. 142.

2. K. Venkata Ramanan, *Nāgārjuna's Philosophy as Presented in the mahā-Prajñāpāramitā-Śāstra* (Bharatiya Vidya Prakashan, 1971), p. 109.

3. Ibid., p. 38.

I	II
X precedes Y Duality precedes power	(Y precedes X) Power preceds or is concurrent with Duality
III	**IV**
X precedes and does not precede Y Duality both precedes and does not precede power	(X precedes or not precedes Y) Duality neither precedes nor does not precede power

We have given brief discussions of where the contradictions arise in views I and II, and we will leave it to the reader to extend the analysis to views III and IV. It is clear then that any view of power is misleading if taken as ultimately true.

We hope that this play of concepts against each other will give some notion of "power" in the world of Don Juan. Power permeates Don Juan's teachings from beginning to end. And in view of so many connections drawn by Don Juan between power and our world, no amount of paraphrasing can relay the impact of Don Juan's message. For this reason we shall now leave the intellectual analysis of the notion of power in order to achieve a more poetic understanding of power. However, this poetry has a most unusual source and does not read in rhyme.

* * * *

The base to which we refer above as a poetic counterpoint to the rigors of the dialectic is Einstein's general theory of relativity, and in particular as it refers to the phenomenon of black holes. Without going into the mathematical details[1] of the theory of black holes, we shall take an intuitive approach to the subject.

A black hole is simply a star that has collapsed into a very small diameter. This collapse is the result of eons of "nuclear aging" of the star. There are other prerequisites; one of them is that the star itself before collapse must be approximately two to three times the diameter (and therefore 27 times the volume) of our sun. Upon fulfilment of these prerequisites the star

1. Refer esp. to P. A. M. Dirac, *General Theory of Relativity* (New York : John Wiley and Sons, 1975).

collapses into a volume with a diameter roughly of the order of two miles. That is to say that a star with a mass of 27 times greater than the sun inhabits a volume whose diameter measures but the distance of a short walk. The magnitude is staggering when we consider that our own earth is nearly a grain of sand compared to our own sun.

With such a concentration of mass in a small volume, stupendous gravitational forces ensue. So gigantic is this gravitational force that even photons cannot escape, and therefore the name, "black hole."

In addition to this, any object falling into the black hole would require an infinite amount of time to do so when the event is observed from our own inertial framework (earth). However, when viewed from the inertial framework of the object moving toward the black hole, the event of entering the black hole actually takes place within a finite amount of time. According to Dirac :

> We see that the Schwarzschild solution for empty space can be extended to the region of $r < 2m$. But this region cannot communicate with the space for which $r > 2m$. Any signal, even a light signal, would take an infinite time to cross the boundary $r = 2m$, as we can easily check. Thus we cannot have direct observational knowledge of the region $r < 2m$. Such a region is called a black hole, because, things may fall into it (taking an infinite time, by our clocks, to do so) but nothing can come out.
>
> The question arises whether such a region can actually exist. All we can say definitely is that the Einstein equations allow it. A massive stellar object may collapse to a very small radius and the gravitational forces then become so strong that no known physical forces can hold them in check and prevent further collapse. It would seem that it would have to collapse into a black hole. It would take an infinite time to do so by our clocks, but only a finite time relatively to the collapsing matter itself.[1]

1. P. A. M. Dirac, *General Theory of Relativity* (New York : John Wiley and Sons, 1975), pp. 35-36.

Thus according to Einstein and Dirac there are events which could take place when viewed from the point of the object in question, and that are quite impossible by our own measurement since an infinite amount of time would be required for their fulfilment.

Suspected black holes have since been observed. They emit random x-radiation, among others, and are thereby detectable. However, they do not seem to coincide with our notions of conservation of mass and energy.

Actually Einstein's theory only approximates coincidence with our everyday conceptual framework in a certain segment of electromagnetic phenomena, namely low velocities or static bodies.[1] In these instances, our lines are straight (Euclidean three-dimensional geometry) and events can happen (i.e. cause and effect in a limited time). Outside of this framework, i.e. among higher velocities approaching light and larger masses in motion, our notion of the universe "warps." That is, according to Dirac,

> One can easily imagine a curved two-dimensioal space as a surface immersed in Euclidean three-dimensional space. In the same way, one can have a curved four-dimensional space immersed in a flat space of a larger number of dimensions. Such a curved space is called a Riemann space. A small region of it is approximately flat.
>
> Einstein assumed that physical space is of this nature and thereby laid the foundation for his theory of gravitation.[2]

Let us then follow a thought experiment using the rules of Riemannian space and Einstein's conception of the world. Let us put a small friend on an electron and let him travel toward a black hole. According to Einstein, space is curvilinear in the respect that one must travel (from our frame of reference) upon a curved "track" when travelling from regions of "empty" space (a place where only gravitational fields exist)[3] to or

1. P. A. M. Dirac, *General Theory of Relativity* (New York : John Wiley and Sons 1975), pp. 30-32, see Schwarzschild solution.
2. Ibid., p. 9.
3. Ibid., p. 25.

through areas near matter and or energy sources. So, according to our inertial framework, as our friend traverses through space, he travels on one of many hyperbolic paths that converge as one nears the vicinity of matter, and diverge as one vacates the premises. According to our friend, *he* is travelling straight through space and particles close to or identical with our inertial framework are moving on these strange hyperbolic curves. As if this weren't enough, as our friend is merrily sailing toward the black hole, our tensions mount even more, because according to us, the event could never happen, and yet according to him, he will be arriving at exactly 10:53 a.m. EST (he knows because our friend is an extremely short, sharp physicist). According to Dirac,

> Thus, as $r \rightarrow 2m$, $t \rightarrow \infty$. The particle takes an infinite time to reach the critical radius $r = 2m$.
>
> Let us suppose the particle is emitting light of a certain spectral line, and is being observed by someone at a large value of r. The light is red-shifted by a factor $g_{00}^{-1/2} = (1\text{-}2m/r)^{-1/2}$. This factor becomes infinite as the particle approached the critical radius. All physical processes on the particle will be observed to be going more slowly as it approaches $r = 2m$.
>
> Now consider an observer travelling with the particle. His time scale is measured by ds. Now
>
> $$\frac{ds}{dr} = \frac{1}{v^1} = \left[k^2 - 1 + \frac{2m}{r}\right]^{\frac{1}{2}},$$
>
> and this tends to $-k^{-1}$ as r tends to 2m. Thus the particle reaches $r = 2m$ after the lapse of finite proper time for the observer. The travelling observer has aged only a finite amount when he reaches $r = 2m$. What will happen to him afterwards? He may continue sailing through empty space into smaller values of r.[1]

So our friend may travel into the black hole, but we would never know it, because in our life time, and in our inertial

1. P. A. M. Dirac, *General Theory of Relativity* (New York : John Wiley and Sons, 1975). pp. 34-35.

framework according to Einstein, he would be travelling on an infinitely long curved track. Infinitely long, because travelling at those rates in or out of the vicinity of a black hole slows down time to such an extent as to approach infinity. We view time elapsed on a graph as approching zero as the velocity of a particle approaches the speed of light.

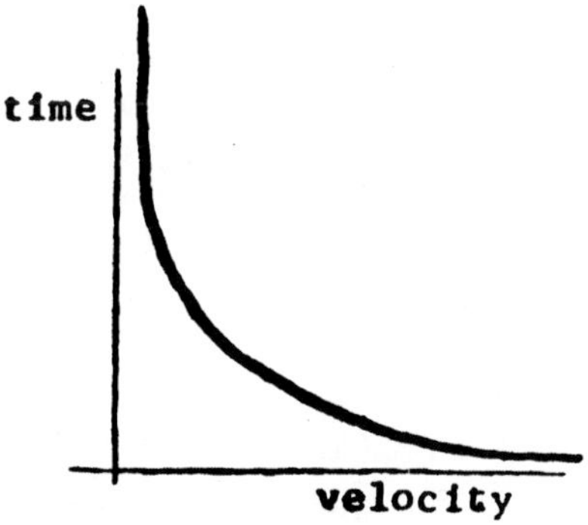

In this instance as well as in Einsteinian equations, the graph approaches the X–axis, but can never quite make it since the energy required to raise a particle (what's more a friend) from our inertial framework to the velocity of light is infinite.

$$E = mc^2 \text{ where } m = \frac{mo\ v^2}{1 - \frac{v^2}{c^2}}$$

where : mo = rest mass (i.e. mass in our inertial framework)
v = friend's velocity
c = velocity of light

As one can see, as $v \rightarrow c$, the denominator approaches zero. This would make $E \rightarrow$ infinity. Conversely, as $V \rightarrow$ small values, the denominator approaches 1, approximating Newtonian motion.

Riemannian space and Einsteinian physics open up new worlds for us. Visualize a particle travelling toward a black hole. Our conceptual framework denies the possibility and this is exhibited by Einstein by his equations involving the impossibility of our observing the event. Visualize a particle slowing and slowing (hyperbolically) as it approaches a black hole. On the one hand, our conceptual network (i.e. Einstein's mathematical description of *his* conception of the universe) tugs and tugs to make certain events grind to halt. Einstein also suggests, however, that according to the clock of our short friend, the time is finite. The only difference between us and our friend is that *we think* he is travelling away from us at a high rate of speed. I say that "we think" he is travelling away because an unbiased observer in a different inertial framework might view the opposite, i.e. that we are travelling away from him (our short friend). Motion is only relative, but when concretized in an absolute framework, our (and Einstein's) mathematics and therefore conceptual frameworks insist the event never occurs. This is no shortcoming of Einsteinian physics, for after all Einstein could see the event from also the particle's point of view in which our point of view seems warped.

In our thought experiment then, we can go only so far (close to the event horizon beyond which, we cannot even conceive of motion). Mathematics is limited by the conceptual environs in which it developed. A breakdown in mathematics such as takes place in the case of time dilation is surely indicative of our conceptual point of no return. Our (Einstein's) mathematics tells us this time grinds to a halt just short of a particle's entrance into the black hole. In addition, the black hole is so small that it has passed the stage (pulsar or neutron star) where the electron has compressed into the nucleus of any atom. This suggests that the notion of space has completely been nullified. After all, there is literally no space between atoms. Objects lose their identity.

> Everything falling into a black hole loses its identity. You do not know whether it was a space probe or a TV set that fell in.[1]

This is so because we could not tell anything of any object that entered the black hole, since there is no way to obtain any information of the object after it has entered the hole. Of course, the notion of cause and effect must disappear since causation lives and breathes duality as well as time. Of course, counter theories may be offered against Einstein's, since any theory must admit

1. Harry L. Shipman, *Black Holes, Quasars, and the Universe* (Boston : Houghton Mifflin Company, 1976), p. 81.

these. However, the theoretical nature of Einstein's work does not in the least detract from his intellectual journey to the boundaries of logic (mathematics). One can only applaud the efforts in carrying studies to the limits without being deterred.

What is the main factor in this non-deterrance ? It is simply the fact that in his study of relativity, Einstein did not tie relative motion as motion being relative to some fixed framework. Relativity comes into play only between *two* objects (inertial frameworks). These objects themselves are relative to others, ad infinitum. This conception of duality is shared with Nāgārjuna who showed the limits of this duality via the prasaṅga (dialectic). Things are relative, but relative to each other and not some third, static framework. This being the case, Einstein can well afford to let his "vision" carry to the logical extreme where duality breaks down. Nāgārjuna does this very same thing by carrying the dialectic to its ultimate end, namely, contradiction.

It is not that the event of the actual penetration into a black hole cannot happen, it is simply that the event cannot be even conceived of in our inertial (conceptual) framework. We cannot conceptually know what it is to achieve the velocity of light since the achievement would require infinite energy; and within our present conceptual boundaries, we are hardly able to discuss what an infinite amount of energy could even mean. Since we cannot conceptually achieve this energy, there is no way for us to view the approach of an object to a black hole as anything but a frozen non-event. The black hole is where concepts (space, time and all) disintegrate. Conceptual disintegration is exactly Don Juan's tool for "stopping the world", "seeing", and experiencing power. Nāgārjuna also makes this point completely clear in his insistence that the dialectic is the starting point for those interested in experiencing modes of consciousness beyond our own.

* * * *

How does this discussion then practically relate to Don Juan's notion of power ? The answer comes in the form of double star. Soon after the interest in black holes erupted, it was decided that due to the elusive, if not vacuous, nature of the black hole the best way to find one would be in combination with another star, i.e. in a two star system. This seemed reasonable since the telltale sign of such an incredibly powerful gravitational sink would be a very "red shift" in the spectrum of the second star. This "red shift" is due to the Doppler effect, according to which the energy of escaping photons (escaping from the second star) is decreased by a gravitational effect. This loss of energy is exhibited on a spectrometer by the shifting of the spectral lines toward the red (lower energy) portion of the spectrum. Presently our most likely experimental subject is the star Cygnus 1. The Doppler shift indicates Cygnus 1 has a mate which has a mass on the order of eight times that of the sun. Yet to date, the mate is invisible. This, of course, is not conclusive, but linked with the fact that Cygnus 1 is a strong x-ray source (only possible with white dwarfs, neutron stars and black holes); and there seems to be an "energy suction" between Cygnus 1 and its invisible mate, all this suggest a black hole.[1] None of this adds up to the proof of the existence of a black hole in the vicinity of Cygnus 1; nonetheless, we can build a modus operandi of a black hole via a model (or thought experiment). It is the model of Cygnus 1 that shall centralize our poetic discussion of power.

The magnitude of a double star system is enormous. The entire happening would spread over a space much larger than our solar system. At the same time, while the event is so large that when one of the stars is considered a black hole, two incredibly mysterious events are observed when photons are literally sucked from the solar star by the black hole. One is that the particulates involved, photons, are completely mysterious when viewed relativistically (see relativistic quantum mechanics). The second is that as mysterious as these entities are, they are not as mysterious as the entity (nonentity) which they approach inside of which space, time and all duality cease. In light of this, let us form a vision of this doublet. At one pole we have an ordinary star, the source of pure energy (light). At the other end we have its exact opposite, the gaping black

1. Kip S. Thorne, "The Search for Black Holes," *Scientific American* (December, 1974), Vol. 231, No. 6, p. 33 ff.

hole which consumes all energy without a trace (x-rays excluded). Between the poles we have a constant flow of electrons from the star to the black hole. From our perspective these photons follow certain "tracks" along a hyperbolic route of space and time or space-time as Einstein prefers. Incredible amounts of energy are involved. Vast portions of space are covered. And yet, in a way, the process is extremely simple. Pure energy traversing enormous space only to be consumed by the nothingness of the black hole. Further than this, the picture is in a way clear and undistorted. This entire scenario depicts something very primordial. So primordial that a full physical description is impossible from our framework. All that we can envision is an enormous flow of mysterious energy upon lines or "track." Einstein refers to these lines as "world lines."[1] Don Juan also refers to lines, lines which he calls "lines of the world."[2] We can think of these lines and energy flow through the help of Einstein's theories, and yet if we try to nail down the whole process, we arrive at a deadend produced by our conceptual framework, and thereby our logic and mathematics. This is a point that makes the physicist cringe, but it enables the student of Don Juan's path to rejoice. The physicist is stymied, but for one who is not concerned with trancendence related to logic, the picture which this doublet creates is marvelous. All conceptual baggage is dropped and we are left with this incredibly vast, beautiful and mysterious display of primordial power. By the way, we should like to insert at this point a quote from Alexandra David Neel's *Magic and Mystery in Tibet,* in order to give the non-Western comparison that we are trying to achieve. Ms. Neel trecked the farthest outposts in Tibet seeking gurus all the way. She describes many fantastic experiences that are reminiscent of the teachings of Don Juan. This is what she concludes about experiencing these lines of the world.

> Now, volitional perfect concentration of mind on one single object, until every other object vanishes from the

1. P.A.M. Dirac, *General Theory of Relativity* (New York : John Wiley and Sons, 1975), pp. 46-47.
2. Carlos Castaneda, *Journey to Ixtlan* (New York : Simon and Schuster· 1972), p. 193 ff.

> field of consciousness, is the basis of the lamaist spiritual training, and this training also includes psychic exercises that aid at developing the power of detecting the various 'currents of energy' that are crossing each other in every direction.[1]

Can more be said scientifically about the black hole ? Most assuredly, but it should be kept in mind that our logic will not penetrate that contradictory singularity known as the black hole. On the outskirts of physics and mathematics lies the last conceptual rock from which we can only take the non-conceptual plunge. Outside of the event horizon duality and time hold for the observer although time is slowed and space is warped. Our conceptual-mathematical framework will only allow that much concession. Beyond the event horizon (impossible for the observer, but possible for the traveller) duality ceases. And therefore our mathematical description ceases because even our most esoteric, the energy tensor, comes in pairs. Where duality ceases, so does the tensor.

In terms of Nāgārjuna, the black hole would signify "emptiness", "emptiness" not in a morbid way, but only in the sense that duality ceases. As would be suspected, though, the black hole is still conceptual and as any other concept can be only dependently originating with yet another concept. It is not surprising then that to date and probably in the future, from our framework (inertial or conceptual) the black hole can only be studied and described with reference to other objects as in the case of the double star.

1. Alexandra David-Neel, *Magic and Mystery in Tibet* (Baltimore : Penguin Books, Inc., 1971) p. 231.

CHAPTER VIII

FREEDOM AND SOTERIOLOGY IN DON JUAN

> 'In the life of a warrior there is only one thing, one issue alone which is really undecided: how far one can go on the path of knowledge and power. That is an issue which is open and no one can predict its outcome. I once told you that the freedom a warrior has either to act impeccably or to act like a nincompoop. Impeccability is indeed the only act which is free and thus the true measure of a warrior's spirit.'[1]

Still, the notion of a warrior and the warrior's connection to the entire picture might be puzzling. If this is so, possibly we can tie up all loose ends with the following discussion.

The warrior is not a warrior in the cowboys and Indians sense. That is to say that even though the warrior could, under special circumstances, be militant and do so impeccably as anything else he may choose, the notion of "warrior" has an esoteric sense which far overshadows that narrow and violent extreme. This notion of warrior has to do not with interhuman struggles, but with the struggle *within* the warrior himself, the struggle between false senses of the self—for example, the tension which is imagined to exist between two thought constructions, "id" and "ego," or "ego" and "superego."

These conflicts are real in that they have effects on our lives. We dissipate energy as a result of these conflicts. And yet, we say that these psychological divisions that we make are "false senses" of the self. This implies an unreality. We seem to reach here an incompatibility.

---

1. Carlos Castaneda, *Tales of Power* (New York : Simon and Schuster, 1974), p. 243.

This is not actually the case. Let us explain. These divisions, id, ego, etc., can be overcome to form one harmonious unit known as the "tonal." The only way to exchange this "real" suffering (enbattlement) for harmony and make the tension an "unreal" memory is to lead the life of a warrior. The warrior understands the notion of "power" and can by virtue of his unclinging ways, deal with power's incarnations. The id, ego, etc., are the incarnations of power. Another way to say this is that the tension that exists between the poles, e.g. ego-superego, is more generically, or even *most* generically power. We conceptualize or incarnate the power as tension, and then invent the poles, since our conceptualization is tinged, or powered, by our clingings. In this context, it is the clinging to these notions of "I."

The warrior knows that conceptualization is illusion because he knows of realms in which such divisions do not have the slightest place. The warrior experiences power which is neither good nor bad nor in conflict with anything.

The warrior knows thought (conceptualization) as "real" in that it has an impact upon our phenomenal life. The warrior also knows conceptualization as "illusion" in the sense that it can be overcome, transcended to achieve new vistas much more generic than any experience which language could afford. Conceptualization is "real", but not ultimately so; conceptualization is illusion, but also not ultimately so. Conceptualization is indescribable since to do so would involve describing it in terms which *should* transcend its own boundaries. Yet this is a priori impossible since any discussion would necessarily include exclusively terms which fall within the boundaries of language. Were this not the case, how could we understand the explanation ?

The warrior explores these fringes of thought and does not become afraid. He realizes that language and thought go only so far, and from then on, we are on our own. The question then immediately arises, "Isn't it obvious that the warrior has changed during the course of his apprenticeship?" One might quickly jump to say "Obviously so !" As might be suspected, our answer is that this is only a view. A view with a certain degree of phenomenal validity, but nonetheless, it is a view.

It is the purpose of this chapter to deal with the notion of change. Presently in our western society there is a strange notion of change. Unfortunately, our western religions have done nothing to alleviate the difficulty. The notion of change to which we refer is the idea that one should eliminate those aspects of our personality which we and or others deem "bad." This personal change is then amputating a section of the personality with the slack being taken up either by expanding another portion of the self or transplanting an "alien" aspect. For instance, a religious counselor might tell an extremely curious and gossipy client to drop these habits and substitute prayer.

While this sort of advice may be well intentioned, it can be further damaging in that the views themselves do not allow certain aspects of the "tonal" to surface at all. The patient then denies an aspect of himself without considering the consequences.

The most prominent of these consequences is the development of the "subconscious". The subconscious is the level where our repressed tendencies lurk in the dark awaiting the innocent passage of its contradictory counterpart in our conscious life. When this happens our consciousness is shaken to the quick. Not being able to contend with the fact that contradictory tendencies can emanate from the same mind, the poor victim is stricken with neurosis. Should this split be taken extremely seriously by the victim, psychosis develops where the person crosses from one rigid set of values to another while meticulously wiping out the memory of the opposite.

We may be forcing neurosis and even psychosis upon ourselves simply by neglecting or attempting to discard aspects of ourselves. Unfortunately these aspects are not realized as part of the self. Or even worse, if they are considered as parts, then the self is considered something that can be partitioned and pieces left out.

This is not to say that, for example, felonious conduct should be an acceptable form of behavior. Quite the contrary. When the roots of our consciousness are found and the dirt shaken off of them for their inspection, the underlying foundation for these felonious examples of neurosis and psychosis are transformed.

These underlying foundations are transformed in the case of a warrior to the extent that there will be no longer any desire to act feloniously towards his fellow man. Rather, the foundations will be rearranged in such a way as to afford alternative plans of action as a personal expression of whatever aspect of the person which was venting its way to freedom through crime.

The subconscious is developed then by us as a place where we can dispose of unwanted refuse. There is no further route of disposal after entering the subconscious over and above our dumping the ejected into our mental garbage can. There being no garbagemen to aid in the psychological recycling, we should not be surprised when the garbage overflows and is infested with all sorts of parasitic pestilence.

For the warrior, nothing (no part of the self) is unwanted and there is therefore no garbage nor garbage can since the warrior accepts himself in total for what he is. The warrior does not try to prune himself down to be what others think he should be. In short, the warrior accepts his conditions, including his personality, as given. He has merely to work with these boundaries or conditions in order to achieve perfection.

If a warrior is jealous, he would admit it to himself, accept it, but not drop it. The warrior would ask himself, "why ?" Of course the answers are not simple, and at most times painful. But the non-clinging life of a warrior prepares him for the shock of encountering the so-called "darker" aspects of the self.

* * * *

In the life of a warrior, the warrior does not change in the above sense of amputation. Rather,

> 'I've already told you that I am in charge of your *tonal* and that Genaro is in charge of your *nagual*,' he went on. 'It has been my duty to help you in every matter concerning your *tonal* and everything that I've done with you or to you was done to accomplish one single task, the task of cleaning and reordering your island of the *tonal*. That's my job as your teacher. Genaro's task as your benefactor is to give you undeniable demonstrations of the *nagual* and to show how to get to it.'
>
> 'What do you mean by cleaning and reordering the island of the *tonal* ?' I asked.

'I mean the total change which I've been telling you about from the first day we met,' he said. 'I've told you countless times that a most drastic change was needed if you wanted to succeed in the path of knowledge. That change is not a change of mood, or attitude, or outlook; that change entails the transformation of the island of the *tonal*. You have accomplished that task.'

'Do you think that I've changed?' I asked.

He hesitated and then laughed loudly.

'You are as idiotic as ever,' he said. 'And yet you're not the same. See what I mean?'[1]

What, then, is the rearranging of the elements of the island of the tonal?

Don Juan pointed out then that there was seemingly a contradiction in the idea of change; on the one hand, the sorcerers' world called for a drastic transformation, and on the other, the sorcerers' explanation said that the island of the 'tonal' was complete and not a single element of it could be removed. Change, then, did not mean obliterating anything but rather altering the use assigned to those elements.

'Take self-pity for instance,' he said. 'There is no way to get rid of it for good; it has a definite place and character in your island, a definite facade which is recognizable. Thus, every time the occasion arises, self-pity becomes active. It has history. If you then change the facade of self-pity, you would have shifted its place of prominence'.

I asked him to explain the meaning of his metaphors, especially the idea of changing facades. I understood it as perhaps the act of playing more than one role at the same time.

'One changes the facade by altering the use of the elements of the island,' he replied. 'Take self-pity again. It was useful to you because you either felt important and

1. Carlos Castaneda, *Tales of Power* (New York : Simon and Schuster, 1974), p. 226-227.

deserving of better conditions, better treatment, or because you are unwilling to assume responsibility for the acts that brought you to the state that elicited self-pity, or because you were incapable of bringing the idea of your impending death to witness your acts and advise you.

'Erasing personal history and its three companion techniques are the sorcerers' means for changing the facade of the elements of the island. For instance, by erasing your personal history, you have denied use to self-pity; in order for self-pity to work you had to feel important, irresponsible, and immortal. When those feelings were altered in some way, it was no longer possible for you to feel sorry for yourself.

'The same was true with all the other elements which you've changed on your island. Without using those four techniques you never could've succeeded in changing them. But changing facades means only that one has assigned a secondary place to a formerly important element. Your self-pity is still a feature of your island; it will be there in the back in the same way that the idea of your impending death, or your humbleness, or your responsibility for your acts were there, without ever being used.'[1]

And so all the elements of the tonal, or for the purposes of our present discussion, the "self" (although the term is *very* misleading), are left intact. The only difference is that their designations of importance have been changed. In this way the warrior's tonal is not the centerpiece of some strange medical theatre for experimental axe-surgery. The tonal is a place where subtle and delicate balancing is practiced on a day to day basis by techniques in mindfulness and so on.

It should be reiterated that the tonal is not the "self," but only so for our present discussion in this very limited case.

After a long period of training, the warrior "shifts" certain characteristics into more or less prominent places. In the case of Castaneda, this took place without his own knowledge. He

1. Carlos Castaneda, *Tales of Power* (New York : Simon and Schuster, 1974), pp. 236-237.

followed the prescribed methods of Don Juan and achieved the results. It is only because Don Juan is an expert in psychology that he was able to affect these transformations in Castaneda without the knowledge of Castaneda. Of course another prerequisite was Castaneda's unbending faith in Don Juan. Otherwise Castaneda would never have suffered the rigors of the teachings.

It is certain that the warrior changes but we cannot use this term "change" without explicating it in terms of the teaching of Don Juan. The warrior changes and yet does not change. Each human being is phenomenologically the same as others by virtue of being human. Yet, also phenomenologically, each human being has a unique individual personality with his or her own unique conditions. These conditions can never be gotten rid of, and should not be repressed. Our conditions should be used by us to our best possible advantage. We can only determine this best possible advantage when neither the conditions nor their denials are clung to. We should neither rejoice in our conditions nor despair in them. We should simply use them as tools for perfection.

* * * *

It could be easy to come to a wholly incorrect view of this entire discussion. One could think that since things are after all beyond our control (especially in the light of the discussion of power), we should not even attempt to change. To conclude that we should not bother to change from the discussion that the-items-of-the-tonal-remain-as-part-and-parcel-of-our-personality is a mistake.

The rearrangement that we refer to of the items on the island of the tonal is change. However, it is no ultimate change. This does not diminish the importance of the necessity for change. Rather it enhances it. The difference between this sort of change and its refusal (denial) lies in whether or not we cling to the elements of the tonal in the first place. This change involves unclinging from the elements of the tonal. In the true light of the Mādhyamika, however, the unclinging itself is not ultimate but yet necessary for achieving Buddhahood (or in terms of Don Juan, realizing "the totality of oneself").

The totality of oneself is not achieved by clinging to the elements of the tonal (analysis). Neither is "totality" reached by clinging to "detachment" from these items. Nor is the "totality" reached by convincing oneself into stagnation since "supposedly things don't change anyhow." The "totality" is reached through admitting change in an important sense and contrasting it with the idea of non-ultimacy on the other hand.

That is to say that the type of change we have been speaking of is necessary in the realization of the totality of oneself. The change is real because the warrior personally transforms from our human lot of anger, greed, jealousy, despair, etc. The warrior transforms himself from a disjointed tonal who cannot feel at ease with the earth and universe, to a fully together, tight tonal who can fluidly glide through the world non-violently and making "no waves." The change is real.

The change is just as truly unreal since the aspects of the tonal, which once held stern reign over the person, are now at the opposite end of the deal. The warrior is so fluid that he can draw from all corners of the tonal's recesses. The warrior's impeccability (non-clingingness) allows this. Were the warrior to cling to any aspect of the self, this action alone is tantamount to the admission that that particular aspect has "control." The warrior is so fluid and so free that he has control over *all* aspects of the tonal. The warrior is truly free. But free only to be impeccable.

This freedom, as well as any concept of freedom, is illusory. We only hope it proper to say that this freedom of the warrior is less illusory than any other. This is so because this freedom is a total exploration into the depths of ourselves. Living the life of a warrior takes us so deep into consciousness that the warrior sees the most primal nature of the connection between self and world, or mind and body. He sees these connections dissolve (into power) and then reinstate themselves. It is in this way that the warrior's conceptions of "self," "change," and "freedom" are less illusory than others, but illusory nonetheless.

'The profoundest of all the verbal instructions on Mahāmudrā is this :

Cast aside all clinging and the essence will at once emerge.

'The core of Mahâmudrā practice consists of two things, non-effort and non-correction. One should know, however, what this non-correction means. The Jetsun Milarepa explained this point very clearly : 'Concerning the practice of non-correction, one should understand three things : If wandering thoughts and desire-passions are not corrected, one will fall into the lower realms. If the Blissfulness, Illumination, and Non-distinction are not corrected one will fall into the Three Realms of Sáṃsāra. Only the immanent Self-mind needs no correction.'[1]

1. Garma C. C. Chang, trans., *The Hundred Thousand Songs of Milarepa* (New York : Harper and Row, 1962), p. 42.

BIBLIOGRAPHY

Beyer, Stephan. *The Buddhist Experience : Sources and Interpretations.* Dickenson Publishing Co., Inc., Encino and Belmont, California, 1974.

Blofeld, John. *The Tantric Mysticism of Tibet.* Causeway Books, New York, 1974.

Brown, Roger. *Words and Things.* The Free Press, New York, 1968.

Capra, Fritjof. *The Tao Physics.* Shambhala Publications, Inc., Berkeley, 1975.

Castaneda, Carlos. *The Teachings of Don Juan : A Yaqui Way of Knowledge.* Pocket Books, New York, 1974.

———. *A Separate Reality.* Pocket Books, New York, 1972.

———. *Journey to Ixtlan.* Pocket Books, New York, 1974.

———. *Tales of Power.* Simon and Schuster, New York, 1974.

Chang, Garma C. C. *The Hundred Thousand Songs of Milarepa.* Harper Colophon Books, New York, 1970.

———. *Teachings of Tibetan Yoga.* The Citadel Press, Secaucus, New Jersey, 1974.

Church, Joseph. *Language and the Discovery of Reality.* Vintage Books, New York, 1966.

Conze, Edward. *Buddhist Wisdom Books.* Harper Torchbooks, New York, 1972.

———. *Buddhism : Its Essence and Development.* Harper Torchbooks, New York, 1959.

———. *Buddhist Thought of India.* Ann Arbor Paperback, Ann Arbor, 1962.

———. *Thirty Years of Buddhist Studies.* The Univ. of South Carolina Press, Columbia, S.C., 1968.

———. *Astasahasrika Prajnaparamita.* The Asiatic Society, Calcutta, 1970.

David-Neel, Alexandra. *The Secret Oral Teachings in Tibetan Buddhist Sects.* City Lights Books, San Francisco, 1967.

———. *Magic and Mystery in Tibet.* Penguin Books, Inc., Baltimore, 1971.

Deussen, Paul. *The Philosophy of the Upanishads.* Dover Publications, New York, 1966.

Deutsch, Eliot. *Advaita Vedanta : A Philosophical Reconstruction.* East-West Center Press, Honolulu, 1969.

Dirac, P.A.M. *General Theory of Relativity.* John Wiley and Sons, Inc., New York, 1975.

Evans-Wentz. W. Y. *Tibet's Great Yogi Milarepa.* Oxford University Press, New York, 1971.

———. *The Tibetan Book of the Dead.* Oxford University Press, New York, 1972.

———. *The Tibetan Book of the Great Liberation.* Oxford University Press, New York, 1972.

———. *Tibetan Yoga and Secret Doctrines.* Oxford University Press, New York, 1974.

Fodor, Jerry A. and Jerrold J. Katz. *The Structure of Language.* Prentice-Hall, Inc. Englewood Cliffs, New Jersey, 1965.

Govinda, Lama Anagarika. *Foundations of Tibetan Mysticism.* Samuel Weiser, Inc., New York, 19[illegible]9.

———. *The Way of the White Clouds.* Shambhala Publications, Inc., Berkeley, 1970.

Guenther, Herbert V. *Treasures on the Tibetan Middle Way.* Shambhala Publications, Inc., Berkeley, 1971.

———. *The Life and Teaching of Naropa.* Oxford University Press, New York, 1974.

Gyatsho, Tenzin. *The Opening of the Wisdom-Eye.* The Theosophical Publishing House, Wheaton, Illinois, 1972.

———. *The Buddhism of Tibet and the Key to the Middle Way.* Harper and Row, New York, 1975.

Hartnack, Justus. *Kant's Theory of Knowledge.* Harcourt, Brace and World, Inc., New York, 1967.

Henle, Paul, ed. *Language, Thought and Culture.* Ann Arbor Paperback, The Univ. of Michigan Press, Ann Arbor, 1965.

Hume, Robert Ernest. *The Thirteen Principal Upanishads.* Oxford Univ. Press, New York, 1971.

Inada, Kenneth K. *Nagarjuna.* The Hokuseido Press, Tokyo, 1970.

Jacobson, Nolan Pliny. *Buddhism The Religion of Analysis*. Southern Illinois Univ. Press, Carbondale and Edwardsville, Illinois, 1970.

Kalish, Donald and Richard Montague. *Logic, Techniques of Formal Reasoning*. Harcourt, Brace and World, Inc., New York, 1964.

Kant, Immanuel. *Prolegomena to Any Future Metaphysics*. The Liberal Arts Press, Inc., Indianapolis and New York, 1950.

———. *Critique of Pure Reason*. St. Martin's Press, New York, 1965.

Koller, John M. *Oriental Philosophies*. Charles Scribner's Sons, New York, 1970.

Korner, S. *Kant*. Penguin Books, Inc., Baltimore, 1970.

———. *Categorial Frameworks*. Barnes and Noble, Inc., New York, 1970.

Murti, T.R.V. *The Central Philosophy of Buddhism*. Allen and Unwin, Ltd., London, 1960.

Poussin, L. de la V. *Madhyamika Karikas of Nagarjuna*. (Bib. Budd. IV).

Puhakka, Kaisa. *Knowledge and Reality*. Motilal Banarsidass, Delhi, 1975.

Puligandla, R. *Fundamentals of Indian Philosophy*. Abingdon Press, Nashville, New York, 1975.

Quine, W. V. *Ontological Relativity and Other Essays*. Columbia Univ. Press, New York, London, 1969.

Ramanan, K. Ventaka. *Nāgārjuna's Philosophy as Presented in the Mahā-Prajñāpāramitā-Śāstra*. Bharatiya Vidya Prakashan, Varanasi, India, 1971.

Rhys Davids, T. W , *Buddhist Suttas*. Dover Publications, Inc., New York, 1969.

Russell, Bertrand. *Our Knowledge of the External World*. Allen and Unwin, Ltd., London, 1969.

Schaff, Adam. *Language and Cognition*. McGraw-Hill Book Co., New York, 1973.

Shipman, Harry L. *Black Holes, Quasars, and the Universe*. Houghton Mifflin Co., Boston, 1976.

Stcherbatsky, F. Th. *Buddhist Logic*, Vol. 1. Dover Publications, Inc., New York, 1962.

———. *Buddhist Logic*, Vol. 2, Dover Publications, Inc., New York, 1962.

———. The *Central Conception of Buddhism*. Motilal Banarsidass, Delhi, 1970.

Suzuki, D. T. *On Indian Mahayana Buddhism*. Harper Torchbooks, New York, 1968.

Taylor, John G. *Black Holes*. Avon Books, New York, 1973.

Thibaut, George. *The Vedanta Sutras of Badarayana*. Dover Publications, Inc., New York, 1962.

———. *The Vedanta Sutras of Badarayana*. Vol. 2. Dover Publications, Inc., New York, 1962.

Zimmer, Heinrich. *Myths and Symbols in Indian Art and Civilization*. Harper Torchbooks, New York, 1962.

———. *The King and the Corpse*. Bollingen Series, Princeton Univ. Press, Princeton, New Jersey, 1971.

———. *Philosophies of India*. Bollingen Series, Princeton Univ. Press, Princeton, New Jersey, 1971.

INDEX